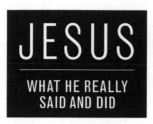

JESUS

WHAT HE REALLY
SAID AND DID

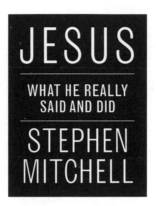

JESUS

WHAT HE REALLY
SAID AND DID

STEPHEN
MITCHELL

HARPERCOLLINS*PUBLISHERS*

Jesus: *What He Really Said and Did*
Text copyright © 2002 by Stephen Mitchell
All rights reserved. No part of this book may be used or
reproduced in any manner whatsoever without written
permission except in the case of brief quotations embodied
in critical articles and reviews. Printed in the United
States of America. For information address HarperCollins
Children's Books, a division of HarperCollins Publishers,
1350 Avenue of the Americas, New York, NY 10019.
www.harperchildrens.com

Library of Congress Cataloging-in-Publication Data
Mitchell, Stephen.
Jesus : what he really said and did / by Stephen Mitchell
p.   cm.
Includes bibliographical references.
Summary: In an insightful look at the life and teachings of
Jesus for teens, respected author and translator Stephen
Mitchell examines commonly held beliefs to arrive at
some essential truths.
ISBN 0-06-623836-6
1. Jesus Christ—Biography—Juvenile literature.   2. Jesus
Christ—Person and offices—Juvenile literature.
[1. Jesus Christ.]   I. Title.
BT302.M63   2002   2001026474
232.9'06—dc21   CIP
                                                      AC

Typography by Hilary Zarycky
1   2   3   4   5   6   7   8   9   10

First Edition

To Lyn Davis Lear

CONTENTS

INTRODUCTION

1

Many people from traditional Christian backgrounds may find this book shocking and offensive. That is understandable. The traditional portrait of Jesus as *the* son of God, who died to redeem humankind from eternal damnation, holds their whole world together. The world wouldn't make sense without it, they think.

I have no quarrel with anyone's religious beliefs. If beliefs about Jesus can help make people kinder human beings, I am in favor of them. My advice to people who think they may be offended by this book is to close it immediately, or better yet, don't open it in the first place.

Other people from Christian backgrounds will find the book shocking but not at all offensive. There is a good kind of shock, which feels like a palmful of cold water on your face when you wake up in the morning. After *The Gospel According to Jesus* (written for adults) was published in 1991, many Christians, and many Jews as well, wrote to tell me how exciting and invigorating my portrait of Jesus seemed. Many of them said that it changed their lives. I was happy for them, happy that they had taken the book in so deeply. I felt we had shared a love for the presence that shines through Jesus' words.

Many people also wrote to ask me how I, a Jew, had come to write about Jesus. I sometimes had to explain that I was not one of the "Jews for Jesus" (Jews who have converted to fundamentalist Christianity). I love Jesus, but I don't believe what most churches say about him, and I don't respect some things that are taught in his name. I love Jesus, but I love the Buddha just as much, and Lao-tzu, and the wisest men and women from all the great spiritual traditions.

Here are a few stories that may help you understand why I wrote that book, and now this one.

2

In September 1952, when I was nine, my parents sent me to a new school. I had been happy at my public school, but my parents wanted to give me a better education. The new school was a private school for boys.

I was a middle-class kid, with a mind full of ordinary nine-year-old things: the New York Giants (not a popular choice in Brooklyn, but my father was a Giants fan), books, comic books, TV, drawing, carving, sleds and ice skates in the winter, animals of all kinds, music. But at my new school something out of the ordinary happened that changed my life. Not outwardly—my parents never knew that there *was* a change. Something happened inside me.

Every Tuesday morning, all the students, from the fifth grade up through the twelfth, attended a Protestant service in the school chapel. We didn't have a choice; attendance was compulsory. I had never been inside a church or chapel before. My parents were Reform Jews. We went to synagogue a few times a year, but the rituals meant nothing to me, and the incomprehensible Hebrew of the prayers and songs sometimes stirred up in my younger brother and me, as we secretly glanced at each other, a surge of giggles that we could barely hold in.

Chapel was different. I liked the hymns. I liked the silences. I didn't understand the Gospel stories and parables, which were read in a dignified, stuffy voice by our headmaster, J. Folwell Scull, Jr., a man for whom I had an instinctive respect and whose name seemed to me a kind of weird poem that contained all the mystery of upper-class WASP America. But the readings touched me. They made me wonder about this Jesus.

They also made me feel guilty. I knew I was Jewish (whatever *that* was), and I suspected that my response to these stories was some kind of disloyalty to my family. So I made a deal with God, or with myself. The deal went like this: It was all right for me to be attracted to Jesus, as long as I didn't recite the words of the Lord's Prayer along with the other boys. If I kept silent, I wasn't really betraying my family.

The deal worked, for five or six weeks. Then one Tuesday morning after chapel—it must have been toward the middle of October—my fifth-grade teacher, Mrs. Commins, took me aside. (Mrs. Commins was the most beautiful woman I had ever seen, and I was in love with her.) She said she had been watching me in chapel during the recitation of the Lord's Prayer. She had noticed that I kept my mouth closed, and she wondered why. I told her that I didn't feel it was right for me to recite the prayer, because I was Jewish. "Oh," she said, "but the words of Jesus are for *all* people."

At that moment something opened in my heart. I

felt that I had been given permission, by someone I loved and trusted, to listen to Jesus. I wasn't being disloyal to my family at all, and it was perfectly all right for me to be Jewish as I listened.

Still, there was a lot in the Gospel passages I heard on those Tuesday mornings that confused me or left me cold. I didn't know if I believed the miracle stories, the walking on water, the loaves and fishes. When I thought about them, my reaction was: "Is this possible? Maybe, but so what?" Of course, it would be cool to learn how to walk on water, but it would also be cool to learn how to water-ski. Anyway, the miracle stories weren't what attracted me to Jesus. What I loved was his kindness and the beauty of his words.

I was more bothered by other things. For example, Jesus talked about forgiveness and loving your enemies. But many of his speeches seemed to be the words of a very angry man, condemning his enemies in violent terms. Then there was the question of heaven and hell. If, as Jesus said, God loves everyone, even the

wicked, how could God send *anyone* to a horrible pun-
ishment that would never end? And what was all this
stuff about Jesus' being "the only-begotten Son of
God"? What did that *mean*? Did it mean that God had
had sex with Jesus' mother? And why did it matter
whether I believed *anything* about Jesus? How could
God reward or punish me for what I believed?

In short, some of the Gospel teachings seemed very
beautiful, even when I didn't understand them. Others
seemed kind of awful. It was all very confusing.

3

But as I grew up, Jesus wasn't a big deal for me, certainly nowhere near as big a deal as baseball was. I
rarely thought of him, and I never read the Gospels
until I went to college. When I did read them, they
were almost as confusing to me as they'd been when I
was nine, and I had the same feelings toward Jesus, of
both attraction and repulsion. It wasn't until much
later that I realized why.

The story of my search for spiritual understanding is too long to tell here, so I will have to fast-forward. I wanted to understand why people suffer so much. I wanted to learn how to be happy: truly happy, not just more-or-less happy. I wanted to find God: not just to believe in God but to actually *experience* God.

I looked everywhere. I read everything I could. I went to famous professors and rabbis. I went to California. I went to Jerusalem for a year.

Nobody knew. People talked a lot and said I should do this or that, but I could tell by their eyes that they didn't really know what I needed to know so badly.

Finally, in 1973, after seven years of searching, I decided to go to India. Other people had met wise teachers there; maybe I would too. But as I was getting ready to leave, a friend suggested that I go to Providence, Rhode Island. There was a Korean monk there, he said, who had arrived in America six months before, with no English and just a hundred dollars in his pocket. The monk had been earning his living repairing washing machines in a laundromat. "He says he's a Zen master," my friend told me. "I don't know if he is, but he has very strange eyes."

So I went to Providence. The Zen master's name was Seung Sahn. He was living in a funky apartment in the poorest section of town. (When I say funky, I mean *very* funky.) There was a big handwritten sign on the door that read WHAT AM I? I walked in and found him sitting at the kitchen table. He was a rotund, very cheerful man in his late forties, with a shaved head, wearing baggy gray pants, a white T-shirt, and a sailor's cap. I looked into his ancient, glittering eyes, and immediately I knew that he knew. He KNEW! I felt that I could walk straight into those eyes and keep walking for miles and miles, and at the end of the path I would meet myself.

I stayed with him and became his student. (I never did get to India.) I began the very difficult spiritual training that Zen provides. I practiced Zen meditation for hours every day. One week out of every month we would meditate together for twelve hours a day. After a year of this, I had an experience in which my mind opened. All my questions about God disappeared. It wasn't so much that I found the answer as that I *became* the answer. Everything was dazzlingly clear. I felt happier than I could ever have imagined. The Zen master was very happy for me.

I stayed with him for many years, deepening my experience and letting more and more light into my mind and heart. I still had a long way to go before earning his complete approval, and earning my own complete approval, and realizing that there was nothing I had to earn. But I was on my path.

4

Fast-forward again. More than a dozen years later I kept having a strong feeling that I needed to write a book about Jesus. There was a magnetic pull. The book was the magnet (even though it didn't exist yet), and I was the piece of iron.

I didn't know what kind of book it would be. I didn't know how long it would take. I just knew that I had to write it.

I had a powerful sense that I could understand Jesus now. It had been more than a dozen years since my inner eye had opened (or since, in Jesus' language, I had "entered the kingdom of God"). I felt that I was seeing the world the way he saw it, the way the Buddha, Lao-tzu, and all the great masters saw it. I was sure that all my confusion about him was a thing of the past.

I began to read the Gospels again. I studied all the scholarship that seemed to me intelligent and open-minded. I polished up my Greek, the language in which the Gospels were written. I learned textual scholarship. And things began to become clear.

The composition of the Gospels is a very complex subject, but in brief here is what I discovered.

Jesus never wrote anything himself. The earliest account we have of him is the Gospel According to

Mark, which dates from around the year 70, forty years after Jesus' death. The Gospels of Matthew and Luke probably date from the decade between 80 and 90, and the Gospel of John probably from between 90 and 100. None of these books was written by a direct disciple of Jesus. Jesus did have disciples named Matthew and John, but they weren't the authors of the Gospels attributed to them. The Gospels were written in Greek, a language Jesus may or may not have known. His language was Aramaic, which is a cousin of Hebrew. His original words, in the original Aramaic, may never have been written down; if they were, they have been lost (except for one word, *abba*, which means "father").

Forty years is a long time; fifty or sixty years is even longer. During these years many stories were told about Jesus, and there were many reports of what he said. Some of the stories and reports were handed down orally from Jesus' own disciples, who lived with him and knew him, even if they didn't always understand his teachings. Other stories and reports were made up much later, by disciples of disciples, who never knew the actual Jesus. Some people faithfully repeated the words he taught, and others added very different teachings, according to their own sense of what was true. When the Gospels came to be written, their authors inherited a mixed collection of teachings and stories, only part of them originating in the life and teachings of Jesus himself.

But could I sort one part from the other? Could I tell the difference between Jesus' authentic words and the words that were put into his mouth later on? I decided to follow the example of Thomas Jefferson. Jefferson, the author of the Declaration of Independence and the third president of the United States, was an extremely intelligent and deeply religious man, and he spent a good deal of time throughout his life thinking about Jesus. Here is what he said: "There is internal evidence that parts [of the Gospels] have proceeded from an extraordinary man, and that other parts come from very inferior minds. It is as easy to separate those parts as to pick out diamonds from dunghills."

The first sentence seemed to me absolutely true. But was it so easy to separate the two parts? Jefferson thought so. In the evening hours of one winter month in the early 1800s, during his first term as president, he began to compile a version of the Gospels that would include only what he considered the authentic accounts and sayings of Jesus. These he snipped out of his King James Bible and pasted onto the pages of a blank book. He took up the project again in 1816, when he was seventy-three, eight years after the end of his second term. The "wee little book," which he entitled *The Life and Morals of Jesus of Nazareth*, remained in his family for a hundred years. In 1904 it was published by order of the Fifty-seventh Congress; a copy was given to each member of the House and Senate. This book, known as the Jefferson Bible, is still in print.

I finally understood why I had been so confused by the Gospels when I was a boy. I had been attracted to

Jesus' authentic words, but I had very much disliked many of the passages that were added later. Some of these passages are actually the direct opposites of his authentic teaching about God's love, like the saying at the end of Mark's Gospel: "Whoever believes and is baptized will be saved, but whoever doesn't believe will be damned." These sayings make Jesus sound ignorant and small-hearted, and they make his God sound like a cruel tyrant. I think that Jesus would have been appalled to hear such words put into his mouth. (Or maybe they would have sounded so absurd to him that he might have been amused.)

For example, Jesus teaches us not to judge (in the sense of not to condemn) but to keep our hearts open to all people; the later "Jesus" is the final Judge, who will float down terribly on the clouds for the world's final rewards and condemnations. Jesus cautions against anger and teaches the love of enemies; the later "Jesus" calls his enemies "children of the Devil" and attacks them with the utmost savageness and contempt. Jesus isn't interested in defining who he is (except for one passing reference to himself as a prophet); the later "Jesus" talks on and on about himself. Jesus speaks of God as a loving father, even to the wicked; the later "Jesus" preaches about a god who will cast the disobedient into everlasting flames. No wonder Jefferson said, with barely contained indignation: "Among the sayings and discourses imputed to him by his biographers, I find many passages of fine imagination, correct morality, and of the most lovely benevolence; and others again of so much ignorance, so much absurdity, so much untruth, charlatanism, and imposture, as to pronounce it impossible that such contradictions should have proceeded from the same being."

So I followed Jefferson's example. But unlike him, I was able to use the precision tools of modern scholarship. I also used the spiritual intuition that I had deepened over many years of Zen training. I selected and translated only those passages that seemed to me authentic accounts and sayings of Jesus, and I left out every passage that seemed like a later addition.

Some of these choices are foolproof. You would have to be pretty dense not to recognize the parables of the Good Samaritan and the Prodigal Son as the words of a great spiritual genius, or the saying about becoming like children if we wish to enter the kingdom of God, or the passages in the Sermon on the Mount that teach us to be like the lilies of the field and to love our enemies so that we may be sons of our Father in heaven. In the same way, there are sayings that all reputable scholars agree could not possibly be authentic. (For example, the saying previously quoted—"Whoever believes and is baptized will be saved, but whoever doesn't believe will be damned"—which doesn't appear in the earliest and best manuscripts of Mark, is known to be an addition by a second-century Christian scribe.) In between, there is a group of sayings and stories that scholars differ about. Selecting among these intermediate sayings is a subjective process, to some extent. I have tried to err on the side of excluding rather than including too much.

Eventually I finished the scholarly work and sat down to write *The Gospel According to Jesus*. But somehow I wasn't ready. Something was missing. I didn't know what that something was, but I knew that I couldn't begin writing. Not yet.

5

One more fast-forward. I went on to other projects but always kept listening and looking for a sign that I should begin writing about Jesus. Then, in 1989, out of the blue, I got a call from a Jewish organization in San Francisco that had awarded me a prize, a generous amount of money, on condition that I spend at least three weeks in Israel. As soon as I heard this, something inside me said, "This must be it. This must be the sign."

So I went to Israel, to Galilee, to take in the sights and sounds that might bring me closer to the real Jesus. At the end of two weeks I was baffled. There were interesting places like the ruins of Capernaum, where Jesus lived for a while; there were places that were hideous, like the garish modern church on the supposed site of the Sermon on the Mount. But nothing seemed to have anything to do with Jesus. Nothing resonated that way for me. I couldn't understand why I was there.

When there was nothing left to visit in Galilee, Shahar, my Israeli guide, persuaded me to accompany him to the Sinai desert for five days. He had lived in the Sinai through most of the seventies, until it was returned to Egypt as part of the Camp David agreement; he had a passionate love for the land and for the Bedouin, and his enthusiasm was contagious. So I said yes. And like a reverse Moses, he led me *into* the land of Egypt.

I soon discovered that the real reason I had gone to Israel this time was to meet Musa, the Bedouin guide we hired to take us into the wilderness. Musa was a true patriarch, and his world was still, in its essence, the world of Abraham, Isaac, and Jacob. I met him in the village of Santa Katerina. He was wearing the white Arab headdress called kaffiyeh, a frayed navy blue Western suit jacket over a tan robe with white pants underneath, cheap plastic sandals, and, on his back, an old khaki knapsack fastened with rope. He was a handsome man, in his mid forties, and looked like Omar Sharif's thinner brother. Like most male Bedouin, he had teeth stained yellow by tobacco and strong tea.

We took off into the mountains. The first time Musa stopped to pray (devout Muslims pray five times a day, bowing to the ground with their whole bodies), I noticed something in his bowing that made me catch my breath. The quality of surrender was extraordinary. It seemed to flow through him from the inside out, out to his toes and fingertips. He was praying with his whole body. His purity of heart was so visible that I felt tears rising in my throat. I wanted to get up and start bowing alongside him, but I thought it would freak him out, and freak out my Israeli friend even more. A Jew bowing to Allah? Too far outside their definitions. So I bowed alongside him in my mind.

The next day we climbed Mount Abbas Pasha and looked out at Jebel Musa (Mount Sinai) and down onto the Plain of Er-Raha (the Rest), where according to tradition the Israelites waited for Moses to come down from Mount Sinai. Late in the afternoon we hiked across Jebel Sumera to Wadi Jebal (the Wadi of the Mountains), a wide granite valley where Musa took us to his garden. It was astonishingly lush: apple trees, apricots, figs, almonds, grapes, olives, pomegranates, quince, plums, and wild peaches. After a few minutes his five children entered. They were dressed in dirty, torn clothing, but their faces were beautiful.

This was the first time I had seen a patriarch in the flesh, and I was astonished. It was as if the word *patriarch*, with all its currently offensive associations, were a photographic negative and had just been printed into its positive form. I felt I was in the presence of an ancient father-king, through whom all the gifts of the earth were being bestowed on his children. He was a huge presence for them: pure generosity, pure creativity, the power that blesses and keeps and makes its face to shine upon all its children. The reverence these children showed Musa was an emotion I had never seen in Western children, and it didn't exclude great affection and good humor between them. As I watched this patriarch with his adoring children, a voice inside me said, "Aha!" This was what Jesus meant by *abba* (father). This was what I needed to understand. At that moment, I knew that as soon as I returned to America I could begin writing.

The book you are about to read is based on the book I wrote then, *The Gospel According to Jesus*. It is a portrait of one of the most beautiful men who ever lived. He himself would probably not have considered himself beautiful or even special. He would have said that we all are beautiful, we all are special, because—and he did say this—we are all children of God.

JESUS

NOTE: In the following text, the Monotype Grotesque Light typeface (it looks like this) indicates that the passage is a direct translation from the Greek of the Gospels. My translations are usually quite literal, but sometimes I have translated more freely or paraphrased in order to clarify a teaching.

If you are a parent, teacher, librarian, or a particularly curious young person who seeks clarification on certain points in the text, you may want to take a look at the Notes on pages 113–145.

WHO WAS JESUS?

Jesus was born and raised a Jew. He thought of himself as a Jewish teacher. All his direct disciples were Jews. He felt that his job was to teach Jews about God and about the right way to live (though his teachings truly are for all people, Jews and Gentiles alike). He remained a Jew throughout his short life. He didn't intend to begin a new religion. He wouldn't even have known what the word *Christian* means. (*Christian* is a word that appeared after his death to describe people who believed some things that he himself never believed.)

Nor would he have recognized the name Jesus Christ. His name was Yeshua or Yeshu (rhymes with *day shoe*), which is Joshua in English and Jesus in Greek. He didn't have a last name. No one did in those days. Men were called So-and-so son of So-and-so, or So-and-so from Such-and-such a place. Anyway, Christ isn't a name; it's a title. It's the Greek word for *mashiakh*, which is a Hebrew word that means "The Anointed One." The Messiah is a figure in Jewish legend, a descendant of the great King David who supposedly will someday appear to make the world perfect. When the Messiah comes (the Jewish prophets imagined), there will be peace and justice everywhere on earth; the land of Israel will no longer be controlled by foreign tyrants; and even fierce animals will be harmless: "[W]olves and lambs shall feed together, and lions shall eat straw like cows."

Jesus once or twice referred to himself as a prophet. But he never thought of himself as the Messiah or as *the* son of God. True, he called God Father, but that was (and is) common in Jewish prayer. He didn't mean that he was literally a son of God. He knew that he had a human father. He didn't think that a male God had come down from the sky and impregnated a human female, who had then given birth to a hero, as in Greek and Roman mythology. What he meant by a son of God was someone who takes after God, just as a son takes after his father. If you truly love God, and treat your fellow human beings with respect and compassion, then you are a son of God. "Blessed are the peacemakers," Jesus once said, "for they will be called sons of God." "Love your enemies, bless those who curse you, do good to those who hate you, and pray for those who mistreat you, so that you may be sons of your Father in heaven." In other words, the more you are *like* God, the more you are a son of God or a daughter of God. Jesus knew that he was not the only son of God. In fact he wanted *everyone* to become a son of God. However poor or stupid or ugly or confused we think we are, all of us are capable of becoming sons or daughters of God. Anyone who acts with unselfish love is God's beloved child. It is equally true that everyone is God's beloved child and that God's love is always present for us, no matter how selfishly we act.

THE POLITICAL SITUATION

Sixty years before Jesus was born, the Romans had con-
quered the whole region of what is now known as
Israel. Over Jesus' lifetime, this region was divided into
three separate countries, each with its own govern-
ment. These Jewish governments under the Romans
were semi-independent. In Judea (where Jerusalem is
located) there was a Roman governor, but the day-to-
day administration was left in the hands of prominent
Jewish citizens. In Galilee, where Jesus lived, the ruler,
Herod Antipas, had to pay an annual tribute to Rome.

He also had to support Roman policies and military actions and maintain public order in his territory. In return, the Romans protected him from invasion by other countries.

The fact that their governments were ultimately controlled by a foreign (and, in their view, godless) power was deeply offensive to many Jews. But the political arrangement was fairly stable. During Jesus' lifetime, there was no real political unrest in Galilee. Indeed, some prominent rabbis thought that the Roman presence was on balance a good thing. "Pray for the welfare of the empire," Rabbi Hanina said, "because if it weren't for the fear of it, men would swallow one another alive." Jesus himself advised people to pay their taxes: "Give to Caesar the things that are Caesar's, and to God the things that are God's."

The rulers had to be very careful, though. The slightest sign of political upheaval seemed dangerous to them. (More than thirty years after Jesus' death, there was in fact a widespread revolt, which the

Romans suppressed with their usual efficiency and ruthlessness; this revolt ended in the destruction of the Temple in the year 70.) Any popular, charismatic preacher was a potential threat. That is why, at the beginning of Jesus' career, Herod Antipas had John the Baptist arrested and executed; he thought that John was creating a political disturbance. And that is probably why Jesus himself was killed.

JESUS' BIRTH AND CHILDHOOD

The story of Christmas, with its angels and wise men, is purely legendary. This beautiful legend was made up by people who loved Jesus and wanted to honor him. The feeling of respect and wonder that we associate with Christmas, and of gratitude to God for his generosity and love, is entirely in keeping with Jesus' teachings. Jesus probably would have liked parts of the Christmas story, especially the saying "Glory to God in the highest, and peace on earth, good will toward men."

The fact is that we know nothing about Jesus' birth and childhood. We know hardly anything about his life before the age of thirty, except that he was a carpenter from the little town of Nazareth in Galilee, to the north of Judea. He was probably born around 4 B.C.E. (Before the Common Era). Some scholars think that he was an illegitimate child—though of course in God's eyes all children are legitimate. His mother's name was Miriam (Mary in English), and he had four brothers—Jacob, Joseph, Judah, and Simon—and at least two sisters. That is all we know. Jesus himself said nothing about his early life.

He was probably poor. Chances are that he learned carpentry from his father (whose name, according to the Christmas legends, was Joseph); trades like this were usually hereditary in the ancient world. But our word *carpenter* is narrower than the corresponding words in Greek and Aramaic, which included such occupations as builder in stone and worker in metal. In all likelihood, as a young man Jesus earned his living building and repairing houses and making farm tools, house parts, and furniture. It is important to understand that his being a carpenter didn't mean that he was uneducated. The level of literacy among Jews at this time was high. It is clear that Jesus' knowledge of the Hebrew Bible was extensive. Though he wasn't a professional scholar, he was a brilliant teacher and more than able to hold his own in debates with learned men.

HIS SPIRITUAL AWAKENING

The first incident in Jesus' life that we know of is his baptism.

At about the age of thirty, Jesus became a disciple of a desert prophet named John the Baptist, who appeared in Judea. John had lived for many years alone in the wilderness, fasting and praying. He had eaten the food of the wilderness: locusts and wild honey. According to the Gospel stories, he dressed in camel's hair, with a belt of animal hide around his waist. His eyes glowed, and he spoke with ferocious intensity.

John said that if Jews confessed their sins and washed themselves clean, God would forgive them, and the whole country would be purified. He said that the world as people knew it was coming to an end. He said that God would soon send his Messiah, a descendant of the great king David, who would lead Jews to victory over the Romans and who would then rule in peace over the land of Israel.

People from all over Israel came to see and hear John. They confessed their sins, and they were washed and blessed by him in the Jordan River. It's probable that many of them felt their spirits renewed.

Jesus went to John and was baptized by him in the Jordan River. We don't know what sins Jesus confessed. They must have been very small. (All the Gospel writers were troubled by this incident when they came to record it. Each of them tried to explain away Jesus' baptism, because they thought that he couldn't possibly have sinned. They believed that he wasn't a fallible human being like the rest of us. I think that Jesus would have been amused by their itchiness.)

As Jesus emerged from the water, he had the kind of experience that is called enlightenment or awakening. Other great teachers throughout history—the Buddha, for example, and Lao-tzu, and the great Sufi and Zen masters—have woken up to reality in the same way. Even today, it is possible to undergo such a profound, life-changing transformation. I am not talking about the usual "born-again" experience, in which people accept the beliefs of fundamentalist Christianity. I am talking about an experience deeper than any belief.

We don't know what actually happened to Jesus during his baptism. But here is my sense of it.

Jesus felt that he had been reborn. It was as if the whole world had dissolved into light. There was a joy in him that he had never known before, a love in his heart that was larger than the world and older than time. He felt absolutely safe and taken care of. He was in God's hands—in God's arms. It was as if God had told him, "You are my beloved child." He knew that the kingdom of God, which the great Jewish prophets had said would come sometime far in the future, was already here. It had always been right here, right now. Nothing could be more intimate. God was nearer than near, and not only to Jesus himself. God's love had always been present in the heart of every person in the world. Everything was always just the way God willed it to be, even when it seemed terrible. Jesus felt as if he were standing at the beginning of the world, as God said, wordlessly, "Behold, it is all very good."

This was a much deeper experience of God than John the Baptist had had. Although Jesus must have been grateful to John, he must have realized, in the weeks and months after his experience, how limited John's teachings were. He must also have realized that for anyone who truly understands, the Messiah has already come. In other words, anyone who stands in God's presence all the time knows that God's kingdom has already arrived.

After his awakening, Jesus went out into the wilderness. He stayed there for many weeks all alone, letting his great experience settle and deepen. There are legends about his time in the wilderness, but again we have no direct account from Jesus himself.

When he came back from the wilderness, he learned that John had been killed by Herod Antipas, for stirring up unrest among the people.

Jesus returned to Galilee and settled in the town of Capernaum, near a large lake called the Sea of Galilee. He apparently never worked as a carpenter again. He began the life of a wandering teacher and healer, proclaiming the good news that the kingdom of God was here and now. He was dependent on people's generosity for his food and lodging, much like a renunciate or monk in Hindu and Buddhist countries. In doing this, he was practicing what he preached: "Don't worry about how you will make your living or what you will eat tomorrow. Only trust God, and everything you need will be given to you."

This may seem to you like a very risky way to live. It requires being without any external security at all, knowing with certainty that whatever happens is good. But people who live this way don't *need* anything from the outside. They see the *ordinary* way of living as risky, since it depends on externals that can never give us real happiness or peace. Jesus is telling the literal truth here. When you trust God completely, everything that happens is a gift.

THE FIRST DISCIPLES

The Gospels tell us that Jesus gathered his first disciples in this way:

As he was walking beside the Sea of Galilee, he saw a man named Simon and his brother Andrew casting a fishing net into the lake. Jesus talked with them for a while. When he walked on, they left their nets on the shore and followed him.

Jesus turned and saw them following him and said, "What are you looking for?"

They said to him, "Rabbi,* where do you live?"

He said to them, "Come and see."

So they went and saw where he lived, and they stayed with him from that day on.

Later, he saw James the son of Zebedee and John his brother, who were in their boat fixing their nets. He talked with them for a while, and they left their father Zebedee in the boat with the hired men and followed him.

Eventually Jesus chose twelve main disciples (probably symbolizing the twelve tribes of Israel). The twelve were Simon, whom he later named Peter (which means "rock," in the sense of "as strong or steady as a rock"); James, the son of Zebedee, and John, his brother, whom he named *b'nai-rogez* ("sons of thunder"); Andrew; Philip; Bartholomew; Matthew; Thomas; James, the son of Alphaeus; Thaddaeus; Simon the Zealot†; and Judas Iscariot.

---

*This means "honored sir" or "teacher."

†Freedom fighter; member of a Jewish resistance group

JESUS AS A TEACHER

The first story that the Gospels tell about Jesus' teaching goes like this:

Jesus and his disciples came to the town of Capernaum. On Saturday, the Sabbath, Jesus went into the synagogue and taught. People were astonished at his teaching, because he taught like someone who has authority, and not like the scribes.

In other words, people were astonished because he spoke to them about God from his own experience, not like ordinary preachers, who had no direct experience of God and relied on the authority of the Bible. Jesus always spoke from his heart. He didn't believe; he *knew*.

One of the most important things he ever said was that the kingdom of God is inside everyone. Here is the story:

Someone once asked him, "When will the kingdom of God come?"

He answered, "The kingdom of God doesn't come if you watch for it. It isn't in heaven. It doesn't come only after you die. No one can point and say, 'It is here' or 'It is there.' For the kingdom of God is within you."

Jesus was one of the greatest spiritual teachers who ever lived. Like all great teachers, he inspired people who met him. Many of them looked at him with enormous reverence. His teaching made them feel closer to God. Some of them could sense a kind of radiance around him, not a halo or anything their eyes could see, but a great lightness and joy. They had a deep feeling of peace in his presence. After knowing him, they began to treat other people with more kindness and compassion.

Jesus enjoyed eating and drinking and liked to be around women and children. He laughed easily, and his wit could be very sharp.

He didn't like most rich people, because he thought that they were preoccupied with their possessions and their power. It is very hard to be both rich and compassionate, he thought. It is almost impossible, he once said, for a rich person to enter the kingdom of God.

He also didn't like certain kinds of "religious" people. You may know the type: people who say, "*We* are saved, and *you* are not," or, "Our religion is the only true one, and other religions are false." People like this, Jesus thought, who divide the world into "us" and "them," don't know what they are talking about when they talk about God. God is only an idea to them. They haven't experienced, in their own hearts, God's love for all beings.

The people he most respected were those who acted kindly to everyone they met. Treating your fellow human beings with love and respect is the best way to love God, Jesus taught. He especially loved those who helped the poor and the unfortunate.

Over and over, Jesus taught that God's love is unconditional. This means that there are no preconditions that have to be satisfied in order for God to love you. You don't have to believe anything; you don't even have to believe in God. Jesus taught that God has a deep love for everything on earth: for the sick and the despised, the good and the bad, for weeds as well as flowers, lions as well as lambs. He taught that just as the sun gives light to both the wicked and the good, just as the rain brings nourishment to both the righteous and the unrighteous, so God's compassion embraces all people. When you are ready to receive it, it is there.

JESUS AS A HEALER

A short time after his awakening, Jesus discovered that he had been given the gift of healing. In our age of scientific medicine, spiritual healers are often considered crackpots or phonies. It is true that there are many crackpots and phonies who pretend to heal people. But there are also true healers. True healers are aware that they are not doing anything when they "heal" a patient. It's the patient's mind that is doing the healing. The body follows the mind.

Here is what the Gospels say about Jesus' first healings:

When Jesus, Simon, and Andrew left the synagogue, they went to Simon's house along with James and John. Simon's mother-in-law was in bed with a fever. As soon as they told Jesus about her, he went and took her by the hand and sat with her. Before long the fever left her. She got up and made dinner for them.

Word spread about the healing. That evening, many people who were sick or troubled came to Jesus.

The whole village was gathered at the door. Everyone looked on in wonder as Jesus healed people.

Early in the morning, while it was still dark, he got up and went out to a remote place and prayed there. Simon and his friends searched for him, and when they found him, they said to him, "Everyone is looking for you."

Jesus said to them, "Let's go on to the neighboring villages, so that I can tell everyone the good news there too."

He went through all of Galilee, teaching in their synagogues the good news that God is right here and right now, and healing many diseases.

*   *   *

In one of the villages, a man who had leprosy came and knelt before him and said, "I know that if you want to, you can heal me and make me clean."

Jesus, moved with compassion, stretched out his hand and touched him and said, "I do want it; be healed."

Right away the leprosy was gone.

Jesus said to him, "Show yourself to the priest and go through the proper ritual cleansing that Moses taught."

The man went out and began to talk about it excitedly, and the news spread, until Jesus could no longer go into a village without being mobbed. He had to stay out in the countryside. People came to him from every direction.

Most scholars agree that Jesus actually did perform healings or that healings occurred in his presence. It is important to understand that there were no hospitals or insane asylums in ancient Israel and that the few doctors available were ignorant and expensive. People who got sick physically or mentally had to be taken care of at home, by their own families. This was a difficult job, especially for poor people, who had enough trouble earning a meager living. Very few people were trained to take care of sick relatives. Sometimes taking care of someone who had become sick or insane was simply too much for a family to deal with, and the patient was forced out of his home and left to wander in the streets like an animal. When Jesus came to a town and performed healings, without even charging any money, he must have seemed to these people like an angel from heaven. Of *course* he was mobbed!

Jesus' experience of healing may have been something like this: One by one, as people crowded around him, he put his hands on them and said a few words that made it easier for them to trust him. The healing didn't happen with everyone. Those who were afraid and couldn't trust him weren't healed. But some of those who trusted him felt their illness begin to dissolve. As he put his hands on a sick person, Jesus felt a flow of energy in his body. It gave him great pleasure. There was a deep calm in him and a quiet sense of joy. The energy flowed through his body and out through his hands, and it moved to whatever part of the body the person needed to have healed.

The cures, when they happened, were not miracles, though they must have seemed miraculous to those who were healed. The human mind and body are much more powerful than we think. There are many documented examples of spontaneous healing, in which a patient with an incurable disease suddenly, magically, gets better, for no reason that medical science can explain. Jesus himself said that he wasn't the one who was healing people; it was their own trust—in God and in themselves—that healed them. In fact, when he went to his hometown of Nazareth, he couldn't do any healings, because people didn't trust him.

PARABLES

Jesus sometimes taught people by using parables, which are stories that tell spiritual truths. How can you explain color to someone who is blind or music to someone who is deaf? You can say only, "It is like this . . ." or "It is like that . . ." Parables say that such-and-such a spiritual truth is like such-and-such a common experience that everybody knows. For example, God's love is like a seed: If it is planted in fertile soil and is watered, it grows by itself. Another example: Someone who has found God's love is like someone who has found a rare and expensive pearl that is worth more than anything else in the world. Jesus wanted everyone to understand him. He wanted to make spiritual things as easy and clear as possible, so that simple, uneducated people could understand them. Even so, some of his parables are difficult.

Here are a few of the most important parables:

Jesus went again to the lakeside, and began to teach, and so many people gathered on the shore that he had to get into a boat on the lake. He sat in it, and the whole crowd sat on the shore, up to the water's edge.

He said to the crowd, "God has planted his love in all of us, like a seed. We don't have to do anything to make it grow. It is like a man who plants a seed in the ground: He goes about his business, and day by day the seed sprouts and grows, he doesn't know how. The earth bears fruit by itself, first the stalk, then the ear, then the full grain in the ear. When the grain is ripe, the man goes in with his sickle, because it is harvesttime. In the same way, when God's love ripens inside us, we become kind and loving people."

He also said, "God's love is like a mustard seed, which is smaller than any other seed; but when it grows, it becomes the largest of shrubs, and puts forth large branches, so that the birds of the sky are able to make their nests in its shade."

He also said, "God's love is like yeast, which spreads everywhere in a batch of dough, even if there is fifty pounds of it, until the whole loaf rises. In the same way, there is no part of our life that is not changed when God's love spreads through us."

And he said: "God's love is like a treasure buried in a field, which a man found and buried again; then in his joy he went and sold everything he had and bought that field."

And he said: "Finding God's love is like this: There was a merchant looking for fine pearls, who found one pearl of great price, and he went and sold everything he had and bought it."

Another time, Jesus said, "When you light a lamp, do you put it under a basket or under a bed? No, you put it on a lampstand. When you feel God's love, don't hide it. It should shine out from your heart and give light to everyone around you. The more love you can give, the more you will receive."

HE BEGINS TO TEACH THE WICKED

Jesus felt that he had a special calling to teach the wicked. By "the wicked" he meant those who willfully disobeyed the law and lived for their own selfish pleasure, without any consideration for others. Tax collectors, for example, were considered by all good Jews to be traitors, because they collaborated with the Romans and got rich by oppressing the poor. Jesus felt that if he could spend time with these people and teach them by his words and his example, perhaps they would change their lives.

Another time, Jesus was walking beside the lake, and a crowd gathered around him, and he taught them. As he walked on, he saw Levi the son of Alphaeus sitting at the tax booth where he worked. Jesus talked to him for a while. When Jesus walked on, Levi followed him and became his disciple.

Many people who held the law in contempt began to follow Jesus and to learn from him. Some pious people said to him, "Why do you spend time with prostitutes and traitors?" Jesus said to them, "It isn't the healthy who need a doctor, but the sick. My teaching is not meant for those who are already righteous, but for the wicked."

MORE HEALINGS

The Gospels say that Jesus went through the towns and villages of Galilee, "teaching in their synagogues, and proclaiming the good news of the kingdom of God." The twelve disciples went with him. There were also many other followers and sympathizers. The Gospels mention "certain women whom he had cured of diseases and infirmities: Mary of Magdala, who had been insane, and Joanna the wife of Herod's steward Kooza, and Susannah, and many others, who provided for them out of their own resources." Here are some more stories about his healings.

Jesus' fame spread throughout the surrounding region of Galilee, and people brought the sick on stretchers to wherever they heard he was staying. Whenever he came to a town or village, they would lay down the sick in the marketplace. They brought him those who were suffering from many kinds of diseases and torments, people who thought they were possessed by demons, epileptics, and paralytics, and he healed many of them.

After Jesus returned to Capernaum, people heard that he was at home; and so many gathered in the house that there was no room, not even in front of the door.

As he was teaching, some people brought a paralytic to him, carried by four men. When they couldn't get near him because of the crowd, they made a hole in the roof over the place where Jesus was, and they lowered the mat, with the paralytic lying on it, through the hole.

When Jesus saw how deeply they trusted him, he said to the paralytic, "Stand up, child; take your mat and go home."

The man looked into Jesus' eyes. Then he stood up

and took the mat and walked out of the house in front of everyone. They were all amazed, and gave thanks to God, and said, "We have never seen anything like this!"

JESUS AND HIS FAMILY

As I said before, we know almost nothing about Jesus' family. There is no mention of his father (except in the legends). There is almost no mention of Miriam, his mother. We are told, though, that after his death, or possibly toward the end of his life, Miriam became a follower of his, and his brother Jacob (James in English) became the head of the church in Jerusalem.

But according to a story we can be sure is authentic (it is so shocking that no disciple would have dared to invent it), his family's first reaction to his career as a teacher and healer was disbelief and worry. The Gospel of Mark says, "When his family heard [about all this], they went to seize him, for they said, 'He is out of his mind.'"

What is happening here? We can't be certain of the details, because we don't know what Miriam and Jesus' brothers heard that troubled them so much. Perhaps it had to do with his healings and exorcisms at Capernaum. Perhaps a neighbor had watched one of the treatments and had returned to Nazareth with a frightening report about the strange sounds Jesus had uttered or the physical contortions he had gone through. (Ancient exorcists are known to have screamed, gesticulated, and made bizarre movements.) Or perhaps there were rumors of his incomprehensible teachings: that the pure in heart can actually see God, or that adults should be like children, or that the kingdom of God has already come.

Whatever it was that they heard, they concluded that he had gone insane. And like any responsible family, they were worried about his well-being and wanted to prevent him from harming himself or others. So they went to Capernaum to "seize" him and bring him back home, perhaps to lock him in a room until he regained his sanity.

When Jesus' mother and brothers arrived at Capernaum, he was in a house, teaching, with a crowd of disciples and sympathizers around him. The crowd was so large that Miriam and his brothers couldn't enter, so they sent in a message, asking him to come out. When he was told that they were waiting for him, Jesus' response was, in effect, to disown them. Of course it isn't difficult to see Jesus' point: that he loves those who do God's will more than he loves even his own mother (if she were not to do God's will). Even so, his refusal to invite his mother and his brothers to come inside seems unkind, almost rude. They must have gone back home to Nazareth in sadness and dismay.

This is the only instance in the authentic stories in

which Jesus acts in an unloving way. Many other great spiritual teachers had to make complete breaks with their families in order to follow their own paths. Some had their families' permission; others, like the Buddha, didn't.

We can guess at the reasons why Jesus didn't open his heart to his mother and brothers, but we don't really know.

Jesus went to the lakeside with his disciples, and large crowds from Galilee followed. Many people, hearing about his healings, came to him from Judea as well, and from the regions that bordered on Judea and Galilee. He told the disciples to have a boat ready for him, so that he wouldn't be crushed by the crowd. (He had healed many people, and the crippled and sick were all pressing in on him to touch him.) Then he went into the house; and such a large crowd gathered around him and his disciples that they didn't even have time to eat.

When his family heard about all this, they went to

seize him, for they said, "He is out of his mind."

His mother and his brothers arrived in Capernaum. Standing outside the house, they sent in a message asking for him.

People in the crowd sitting around him said to him, "Your mother and your brothers are outside and want to see you."

Jesus said, "Who are my mother and my brothers?" Looking at those who sat in a circle around him, he said, "*These* are my mother and my brothers. Whoever does the will of God is my brother, and sister, and mother."

STILL MORE HEALINGS

Some of the more rigid people who witnessed Jesus' healings felt threatened by them, because he wasn't doing them in the officially acceptable way. But most people were awed and grateful.

A mute who acted as if he were possessed by demons was brought to Jesus. Jesus touched him kindly and looked into his eyes and said, "You can talk, you know." The man's heart opened, and for the first time he began to speak. All the people who witnessed this were amazed.

But certain priests who had come down from Jerusalem said, "This Jesus must be a black magician if he can control demons. He casts out demons because he has handed himself over to the prince of demons."

Another time, when Jesus had returned by boat from the other side of the lake, a large crowd gathered around him at the shore. One of the leaders of the synagogue came to him and bowed to the ground before him and said, "My twelve-year-old girl is near death; come, I beg of you, put your hands on her and save her life."

Jesus went with him. A large crowd followed and pressed in on him.

There was a woman in the crowd who had been bleeding for a dozen years, and she had been treated by many healers, and had spent all her money, and hadn't gotten better but worse. She had heard about Jesus, and she came up behind him in the crowd and touched his robe, because she thought, "If I touch him, I will be healed." Immediately the bleeding dried up, and she knew in her body that she was cured of the disease.

Jesus felt the healing energy flowing from him, and he turned around in the crowd and said, "Who touched me?"

His disciples said to him, "You see the crowd pressing in on you; why do you ask, 'Who touched me?'"

He looked around to see who had done it.

The woman, overjoyed but frightened because she had touched him without asking, came and bowed down before him and told him the whole truth. Jesus said to her, "Daughter, it is your own trust that has healed you. Go in peace, and be cured of your disease."

When they finally arrived at the leader's house, Jesus found a great commotion, and loud sobbing and wailing. Some people came to the leader of the synagogue and said, "Your daughter is dead. Why bother the rabbi any further?"

Jesus ordered them all out, and he took the child's father and mother and Peter and James and James's brother John, and they went in to where the child was.

He bent over the child and put his hands on her. Then he turned to her parents and said, "Don't be afraid. Trust me. The child is not dead but sleeping."

Then he took her hand and said, "Child, get up." The girl opened her eyes, got up, and began to walk. Her parents were filled with great astonishment. He told them to give her something to eat.

THE SERMON ON THE MOUNT

Jesus' most famous teaching is called the Sermon on the Mount. This sermon never actually took place. It is a collection of various teachings stitched together by the author of the Gospel According to Matthew. The author of the Gospel According to Luke collected a smaller number of teachings and imagined that the sermon was given on a plain.

Many people think that Jesus' teachings in this collection are the most beautiful in the Gospels. Some of the teachings are simple; some are more difficult.

But all of them obviously come from Jesus' deep and powerful love for God and his desire to help people experience this love.

For the sake of clarity, I have divided the Sermon on the Mount into nine sections, each one introduced by the question that Jesus seems to be answering.

1. Which people are the most fortunate?

Large crowds followed him from Galilee and Judea and the lands bordering them. One day, seeing the crowds, he went up onto a hill, and when he had sat down, his disciples gathered around him. And he began to teach them, and said, "Blessed are the humble, for theirs is the kingdom of God.

"Blessed are those who grieve, for they will be comforted.

"Blessed are those who hunger and thirst for righteousness, for they will be filled.

"Blessed are the merciful, for they will receive mercy.

"Blessed are the pure in heart, for they will see God.

"Blessed are the peacemakers, for they will be called sons of God."

2. Is Jesus destroying the Jewish law by being so friendly with those who break the law?

"Don't think that I want to destroy the law; I don't want to destroy the law but to deepen it. What I am teaching you is that unless your righteousness is deeper than the righteousness of pious people, you will not enter the kingdom of God.

"You have heard that it was said to our forefathers, *You shall not murder.* This law is good, as far as it goes. But what I teach is that even someone who hates another human being is in danger of committing murder.

"You have heard that it was said, *You shall not commit adultery.* This law is good, as far as it goes. But what I teach is that any married man who lusts for a woman not his wife is in danger of committing adultery.

"You have heard that it was said, *You shall not perjure yourselves*. This law is good, as far as it goes. But what I teach is that you shouldn't take any oaths at all. Let your 'Yes' mean 'Yes' and your 'No' mean 'No.' If people know that you mean exactly what you say, you won't have to swear to your words.

"You have heard that it was said, *An eye for an eye and a tooth for a tooth*: all damage should be paid for according to its worth. This law is good, as far as it goes. But what I teach is that you should pay even when you have done nothing wrong. Don't resist a wicked man. If anyone hits you on one cheek, turn the other cheek to him also. If anyone wants to sue you and take your shirt, let him have your coat as well. If a Roman soldier forces you into service for one mile, go two miles with him. Give to everyone who asks, and don't refuse anyone who wants to borrow from you.

"You have heard that it was said, *Love your neighbor*

as yourself; in other words, always treat your neighbor with compassion and respect. This law is good, as far as it goes. But what I teach is that you should treat even your enemies with compassion and respect: do good even to those who hate you, bless even those who curse you, and pray even for those who mistreat you. If you do this, you will truly be sons of your Father in heaven; for he makes his sun rise on the wicked and on the good alike, and he sends rain both to the righteous and to the unrighteous.

"If you respect only those who respect you, how are you acting any better than wicked people: don't even the wicked do the same? If you do good only to those who do good to you: don't even the Gentiles do the same? But respect your enemies, and give to everyone, expecting nothing in return; and your reward will be great, and you will truly be sons of God, who is kind even to the ungrateful and the wicked. Therefore be merciful, just as your Father in heaven is merciful."

*   *   *

3. How should people give charity, and how should they pray?

"Be careful not to do your good deeds in public, in order to be seen. When you give charity, don't call attention to it, as pious people do in the synagogues and in the streets, so that other people will see that they are charitable and praise them. But when you give charity, don't let your left hand know what your right hand is doing. Keep your charity a secret; and your Father in heaven, who sees what is secret, will reward you.

"When you pray, don't be like the pious, who love to stand and pray in public, so that people will see them and praise them. But when you pray, go into your inner room and shut the door and pray in secret to your Father; and your Father, who sees what is secret, will reward you.

"In your prayers, don't talk on and on, as the Gentiles do; for they think that unless they use many words they won't be heard. Don't be like them, for your Father knows what you need even before you ask him. But pray like this:

Our Father in heaven,

    hallowed be your name.

May your kingdom come,

    may your will be done

    on earth as it is in heaven.

Give us this day our daily bread,

    and forgive us our wrongs

    as we forgive those who have wronged us.

And do not lead us into temptation,

    but deliver us from evil.

For if you forgive others their offenses, your Father in heaven will forgive you for what you have done wrong."

4. Can't we just go ahead and act in the right way? Why do we need to understand about God's love?

"Your inner eye, your eye of insight, is the lamp of your body. So if your inner eye is clear, your whole body is luminous; but if your inner eye isn't clear, your whole body is dark. If the light in you is darkness, how great that darkness is!"

5. If God's love is in all of us, why do we need teachers?

"Can a blind man lead a blind man? Won't they both fall into a ditch? A disciple follows his teacher until his own inner eye opens. Once the disciple's inner eye opens, he is exactly like his teacher, and he can walk on the right path by himself."

6. How can we stop worrying about the future?

"Ask, and it will be given to you; seek, and you will find; knock, and the door will be opened to you. For everyone who asks, receives; and everyone who seeks, finds; and to all those who knock, the door will be opened.

"What human father, when his child asks for a loaf of bread, will give him a stone; or when he asks for a fish, will give him a snake? If you, then, who are imperfect, know how to give good gifts to your children, how much more will your Father, who is perfect, give good things to those who ask him.

"Therefore I tell you, don't be anxious about what you will eat or what you will wear. Isn't your life more than its food, and your body more than its clothing? Look at the birds of the sky: they neither sow seeds nor reap the grain nor gather it into barns, yet God feeds them. Which of you by thinking can add a day to his life? Why do you worry about clothing? Consider the lilies of the field, how they grow: they neither toil nor spin. Yet I tell you that not even King Solomon in all his glory was robed like one of these.

"Therefore, if God so clothes the grass, which grows in the field today, and tomorrow is thrown into the oven, won't he all the more clothe you? So don't worry about these things and say, 'What will we eat?' or 'What will we wear?' For that is what selfish people seek; and your Father knows that you need these things. But first seek the kingdom of God; and these things will be given to you as well.

"Aren't two sparrows sold for a penny? Yet not one of them falls to the ground apart from your Father. As for you, every hair on your head is numbered. So don't be afraid: you are worth more than many sparrows."

7. What is the best way to open our hearts to other people?

"Don't judge, and you will not be judged. For in the same way that you judge people, you yourself will be judged.

"Why do you condemn the small offense that your neighbor has committed, but don't notice the large offense that you yourself have committed? First correct your own offense, and then you will be able to correct your neighbor's offense.

"So if you don't judge, you will not be judged; if you don't condemn, you will not be condemned; if you forgive, you will be forgiven; if you give, many things will be given to you. For the more you give, the more you will receive.

"Therefore, whatever you want others to do to you, do to them. This is the essence of God's law."

8. Why shouldn't we just care about our own selfish pleasure?

"There are two gates into life, and two paths that people take. The gate of selfish pleasure is wide and easy to go through, and most people choose it, but it leads to great suffering. The gate of spiritual practice is narrow and hard to go through, and few people choose it, but it leads to true happiness. Don't go the way of selfishness. Enter life through the narrow gate."

9. What if we have faith, but can't do what Jesus says?

"What good is it for someone to say that he has faith when he doesn't *act* as if he loves God? Can your faith save you? If a fellow human being is naked and hungry, and you say to him, 'Keep warm, eat well,' and don't give him what he needs, what good is that? What is important is not that you believe me, but that you act according to what I say. Everyone who hears what I say and acts kindly is like a man who built his house upon rock; and the rain fell and the floods came and the winds blew and beat against that house, and it didn't fall, because its foundation was on rock. But everyone who hears what I say and doesn't act kindly is like a man who built his house upon sand; and the rain fell and the floods came and the winds blew and beat against that house, and it fell, and nothing was left of it."

REJECTION IN HIS HOMETOWN

Jesus' townspeople, like his mother and brothers, couldn't accept him as a genuine teacher and healer. They saw him only as he had been: a poor carpenter, with a rumor of illegitimacy about his birth. They didn't see the magnificent human being he had become after his awakening.

Jesus then went to Nazareth, his native town, and his disciples followed him.

When the Sabbath came, he began to teach in the

synagogue, and many people who heard him were bewildered and said, "Where does this fellow come up with such stuff?" and "What makes *him* so wise?" and "How can he be a miracle worker? Isn't this the carpenter, Miriam's bastard, the brother of James, Joseph, Judas, and Simon, and aren't his sisters still living here with us?" And because they saw him in this way, they were unable to believe what he said.

Jesus said, "A prophet is not rejected except in his own town and in his own family and in his own house." And he was unable to do any healings there, because of their disbelief.

This rejection seems to have been a disappointing experience for Jesus, but one he probably learned from. If Jesus was in fact disappointed by the rejection, this shows that he was still attached to his own thoughts about how things should be, that he desired a certain outcome and hadn't yet totally accepted the will of God. "Nothing external can disturb us," the Greek philosopher Epictetus said. "We suffer only when we want things to be different from the way they are." Here is how the fully mature human being acts, according to the ancient Chinese sage Lao-tzu, in his great book, the Tao Te Ching:

> He lets all things come and go
> effortlessly, without desire.
> He never expects results;
> thus he is never disappointed.

HE HEALS A DEAF MAN, A BLIND MAN

Jesus returned from the region of Tyre and went to the Sea of Galilee.

People brought him a man who was deaf and could hardly speak, and they begged him to put his hands on him. Jesus took him aside, away from the crowd, and put his fingers into the man's ears, and spat and touched the man's tongue. Then he looked up into the sky, sighed, and said to him, "Be opened!" Immediately the man's ears were opened, his tongue was released, and he spoke clearly. The people were very astonished.

*   *   *

A woman in the crowd called out to him, "Blessed is the womb that bore you and the breasts that you sucked."

Jesus said, "No: blessed rather are those who hear the word of God and obey it."

Another time, in Bethsaida, people brought a blind man to Jesus and begged Jesus to touch him. He took the blind man by the hand and led him out of the village. Then he spat into his eyes, and put his hands on them, and asked him, "Can you see anything?"

The blind man looked up and said, "I see men, like trees walking."

Jesus later put his hands on the man's eyes again, and the man looked, and his sight was restored, and he could see everything clearly.

AN EXORCISM

Still another time, a man in the crowd said to Jesus, "Rabbi, I have brought you my son; he is possessed by a demon, and when it attacks him, it throws him around, and he foams and grinds his teeth and gets stiff."

They brought the boy to him; and immediately the boy was thrown down violently, and he thrashed around, foaming at the mouth. Jesus asked the father, "How long has this been happening to him?"

The father said, "Since he was a child. The demon has tried to kill him many times, and thrown him into the fire or the water. But if it is possible for you to do anything, take pity on us and help us."

Jesus said to him, "'*If* it is possible'! *Anything* is possible when you believe it is."

The boy's father cried out, "I believe; help my unbelief."

Jesus put his hands on the boy and spoke to him. The boy cried out and went into convulsions, and then became as stiff as a corpse. Most of the people standing there said that he had died. But Jesus took him by the hand and lifted him, and he stood up.

INNOCENCE AND FORGIVENESS

Once, when they were in Capernaum, the disciples asked Jesus, "Who is the greatest in the kingdom of God?"

He called a young child over, and put him in front of them; and taking him in his arms, he said, "Truly I tell you, unless you change your lives and become like children, you can't enter the kingdom of God."

Peter once asked him, "Sir, how often should I forgive my brother if he keeps wronging me?"

Jesus said, "Forgive him seven times a day."

Peter said, "As much as seven times a day?"

Jesus said, "As much as seventy times seven. For even the holiest of us make mistakes. Even the prophets, even after they were filled with the Holy Spirit, made mistakes."

THE GOOD SAMARITAN

This and the Prodigal Son are deservedly the most famous and beloved of Jesus' parables. (*Samaritan* means someone from the region of Samaria, to the south of Galilee and to the north of Judea. Most Jews of that time despised Samaritans.)

Once, a certain scholar stood up and said, "Rabbi, what must I do to gain eternal life?"

Jesus said to him, "What is written in the Torah*?"

---

*The Hebrew Bible

The scholar said, "The Torah says, *You should love the Lord your God with all your heart and with all your soul and with all your strength and with all your mind.* And it also says, *You should love your neighbor as yourself."*

Jesus said, "You have answered correctly. Love God with all your heart, and love your neighbor as yourself. Do this and you will live in eternity."

The scholar said, "But who is my neighbor?"

Jesus said, "Listen to this story. A certain man, while traveling from Jerusalem to Jericho, was attacked by robbers, who stripped him and beat him and left him on the road, half dead. Now a priest happened to be going down that road, and when he saw him, he crossed the road and passed by on the other side. Then a Levite came to that place and saw him and passed by on the other side. Then a Samaritan who was traveling that way saw the man. And when he saw him, he was moved with compassion. He went over to him and bound up his wounds, pouring oil and wine on them, and put him on his own donkey and brought him to an inn and took care of him. On the next day, he took out two silver coins and gave them to the innkeeper and said, 'Take care of this man; and if it costs more than this, I will pay you the rest when I come back.'" Then Jesus said, "Which of these three, do you think, turned out to be a neighbor to that man?"

The scholar said, "The one who treated him with mercy."

Jesus said, "Go then, and act as he did."

THE LOST SHEEP AND THE LOST COIN

Another time, the tax collectors and prostitutes were all crowding around to listen to him. Some pious people standing there grumbled and said, "This fellow shows no respect for law-abiding people, because he welcomes criminals and eats with them."

Jesus told them this parable. "It is like this: If a man has a hundred sheep and one of them wanders off, doesn't he leave the ninety-nine on the hills and go looking for the one that strayed? When he finds it, he is filled with joy, and he puts it on his shoulders and goes home and gathers his friends and neighbors and says to them, 'Rejoice with me: I found my sheep that was lost.'

"Here is another example: If a woman has ten silver coins and loses one of them, doesn't she light a lamp and sweep the house and keep searching until she finds it? When she finds it, she gathers her friends and neighbors and says, 'Rejoice with me: I found the coin that I lost.'

"In just the same way, God rejoices over one wicked person who changes his life and becomes a decent human being."

THE PRODIGAL SON

This is the heart of Jesus' teaching and one of the most beautiful stories ever told. The final, overjoyed statement by the father—"For this son of mine was dead, and he has come back to life; he was lost, and is found"—describes the only kind of resurrection that Jesus ever spoke about.

Then Jesus said, "Listen to this parable: There once was a man who had two sons. The younger one said to him, 'Father, let me have my share of the estate.' So the man divided his property between them. Not many days afterward, the younger son sold his share, and left with the money, and traveled to a distant country. There he got into wild, wasteful habits, and he spent all his money on his own selfish pleasures. At that time a severe famine arose in that country; and he had nothing left. So he went and hired himself out to a citizen of that country, who sent him to his farm to feed the pigs. The young man longed to fill his belly with the husks that the pigs were eating; and no one would give him any food. Finally he came to himself and thought, 'How many of my father's hired men have more than enough to eat, while I am dying of hunger. I will get up and go to my father, and say to him, *Father, I have sinned against God and against you, and I am no longer worthy to be called your son. Let me be like one of your hired men.*' He got up, and went to his father. While he was still a long way off, his father saw him, and was moved with compassion, and ran to him, and threw his arms around him, and kissed him. The son said to him, 'Father, I have sinned against

God and against you, and I am no longer worthy to be called your son.' But the father said to his servants, 'Quick, bring out the best robe we have and put it on him; and put a ring on his hand, and sandals on his feet. Bring the fatted calf, and kill it; and let us eat and make merry. For this son of mine was dead, and he has come back to life; he was lost, and is found.' Then they began to make merry.

"Now the older son had been out in the fields; and on his way home, as he got closer to the house, he heard music and dancing, and he called over one of the servants and asked what was happening. The servant said, 'Your brother has come, and your father has killed the fatted calf, because he has him back safe and sound.' The older son was angry and would not go in. His father came out and tried to soothe him. But the son said, 'Look: all these years I have been working for you, and never have I disobeyed your command. Yet you never even gave me a goat, so that I could feast and make merry with my friends. But now that this son of yours comes back, after wasting your money on whores, you kill the fatted calf for him!' The father said to him, 'Child, you are always with me, and everything I have is yours. But it was proper to make merry and rejoice, for your brother was dead, and he has come back to life; he was lost, and is found.'"

THE DEPARTURE FOR JERUSALEM

We don't know why Jesus left Galilee and went to Jerusalem toward the end of his first year of teaching. Perhaps he wanted, out of pure generosity, to share the good news with the people of Judea as well as with the people of Galilee. Perhaps he thought that it was his duty as a prophet to teach in the holiest of Jewish cities. But he must have known that it was very dangerous to be attracting crowds in the holy city just before the Passover festival, when there were even more soldiers on alert than usual.

Although Judea was governed directly by the Roman prefect, Pontius Pilate, Jerusalem was governed by the Jewish high priest and his council. They had a great deal of authority, though the prefect had the final authority and the sole right to sentence anyone to death. For the major Jewish festivals like Passover, the prefect came to Jerusalem with additional troops to maintain public safety and to make sure that the large crowds didn't get out of hand.

The Gospels tell several probably authentic stories about what happened on the way to Jerusalem.

After this, Jesus left Galilee and entered the territory of Judea.

It was close to the festival of Passover. Large crowds gathered around him, and he healed and taught.

Some people were bringing children to him, for him to bless; but the disciples rebuked them. When Jesus saw this, he said to them, "Let the children come to me, don't try to stop them; for the kingdom of God belongs to such as these. Whoever doesn't trust God as simply as a child does cannot be filled with God's love." He took them in his arms, and put his hands on them, and blessed them.

One day, as Jesus was setting out, a man ran up and fell on his knees before him, and said, "Good Rabbi, what must I do to gain eternal life?"

Jesus said to him, "Why do you call me good? I am not perfectly good; no one is perfectly good except God alone. You know the commandments: *Do not murder, Do not commit adultery, Do not steal, Do not bear false witness, Do not defraud, Honor your father and mother.*"

The man said, "Rabbi, all these I have kept since I was a boy."

Jesus, looking at him, loved him, and said, "There is one thing that you lack: go, sell everything you have and give it to the poor, and you will find a far greater treasure. Then come and stay with me."

But when he heard this, his face clouded over, and he

went away sick at heart, for he was a man who had large estates.

Jesus looked around at his disciples and said, "Children, how hard it is for the rich to enter the kingdom of God. It is easier for a camel to go through the eye of a needle than for a rich man to enter the kingdom of God."

A second rich man, who had been listening, said to Jesus, "Sir, I too have kept all the commandments. But the Torah doesn't command me to give away my money."

Jesus said, "How can you say, 'I have kept all the commandments'? Isn't it written in the Torah, *You should love your neighbor as yourself*? Yet many of your countrymen are dressed in rags and dying of hunger, while your house is filled with abundance, and none of it goes out to them."

LEAVING THE FAMILY

We all have to leave our parents at a certain point—that is an important part of growing up and becoming independent. But in the following stories, Jesus is talking about a kind of inner leave-taking. If we want to become who we are truly meant to be, we have to free ourselves from our families' desires (who *they* want us to be) and expectations (who they think we *should* be). The only thing we need to follow is our own inner light.

Jesus did, in the previous story, mention the commandment to honor your father and mother. But more often, when he talked about the family, he referred to it as an obstacle. Once he even went so far as to say, "If anyone comes to me and doesn't hate his own father and mother and wife and children and brothers and sisters, yes, and even his own life, he can't be my disciple" (Luke 14:26). Leave your family behind, he usually taught, if you really want to do God's will. It isn't clear whether he meant that people should leave their families behind physically or just in their minds. But however he meant this advice, it is clear that he was speaking from his own powerful experience.

When Jesus says, "Let the dead bury their dead," he means "Let the spiritually dead bury the physically dead; don't bother with such things as ceremonies that are sacred to the family, even ceremonies as important as funerals; just pay attention to God." This is a harsh thing to say to a man whose father has just died. But Jesus wasn't in the mood to be tactful. Perhaps he felt that his own life was coming to a climax. Certainly we can hear the urgency in his words.

As Jesus was traveling along the road, he said to a certain man, "Come with me."

The man said, "Let me first go and bury my father."

But Jesus said to him, "Let the dead bury their dead."

Another man said to Jesus, "I will come with you, sir, but let me first say goodbye to my family."

Jesus said to him, "No one who puts his hand to the plow and then looks back is ready for the kingdom of God."

FIRST DAYS IN JERUSALEM

The Gospels report that there were many rumors about Jesus as he entered Jerusalem. This seems probable. Any powerful teacher and healer who attracted large crowds would have caused people to wonder who he was. Jesus may not have heard the rumors. If he did, we don't know how he responded to them.

As they came near Jerusalem, to Bethany and Bethphage and the Mount of Olives, some people in the large crowds coming for the festival spread their cloaks in front of him on the road, and some people spread brushwood that they had cut in the fields. Those who walked in front of him and those who followed shouted, "Blessed is he who comes in the name of the Lord; praise God in the highest heavens!"

When he entered Jerusalem, some people said, "This is the prophet Jesus, from Nazareth in Galilee." Other people said, "He is a great healer." Other people said, "He must be the Messiah, the King of the Jews. He will lead us to victory over the Romans." Many people were stirred up, wondering who he was.

He entered the Temple and looked around at everything; but since it was already late, he went out to Bethany with the twelve disciples.

Every day Jesus would go to the Temple to teach, and at night he would stay on the Mount of Olives. Early in the morning he would go back into the Temple, and many people gathered around him. He sat and taught them, and they listened to him with delight.

TAXES TO THE EMPEROR

The following stories took place during Jesus' final days of teaching. The issue in this story was an important one for many Jews: Should they support the Roman Empire by paying their taxes (and thus undermine the cause of Jewish nationalism), or should they refuse to pay taxes (and thus be liable to severe penalties)? The scholars may have been trying to trick Jesus into taking one or the other side of this difficult issue. But the question may just as well have been sincere.

One day, as he was teaching in the Temple, some scholars said to him, "Rabbi, is it lawful to pay the tax to Caesar, or not?"

Jesus said, "Bring me a coin."

They brought one. He said, "Whose image is on it?"

They said, "Caesar's."

Jesus said, "Give to Caesar the things that are Caesar's, and to God the things that are God's."

THE GREATEST COMMANDMENT

The scholar in the following beautiful dialogue is a sincere seeker of God's kingdom. He asks his question because he so greatly admires, or is so deeply touched by, Jesus' teaching. It is not a naive question, asked out of ignorance and hunger for the truth; it is a kind of test, but a sympathetic one, without a trace of hostility. The scribe wants to know, for his own sake, how well Jesus can do with this essential question. Jesus' answer—especially his statement that "On these two commandments all the Torah and the prophets depend"—is extremely powerful, and the scholar responds to it with wholehearted enthusiasm.

Jesus is delighted by the quality of the scholar's response. From the scholar's excited, loving approval, Jesus can see into his heart. The scholar is not far from the kingdom of God. In fact, once he takes a few more steps toward it, he will realize that he has been inside it all along.

Later, a certain scholar, who had been listening to Jesus and had observed how well he answered people's questions, asked him, "Which commandment is the greatest of all?"

Jesus answered, *"Hear, O Israel: the Lord our God is one; and you shall love the Lord your God with all your heart and with all your soul and with all your mind and with all your strength.* This is the first and greatest commandment. And there is a second one that is like it: *You shall love your neighbor as yourself.* On these two commandments all the Torah and the prophets depend."

The scholar said to him, "Excellent, Rabbi! You have said the truth, that God is one and there is no other beside him, and to love him with all your heart and all your understanding and all your strength, and to love your neighbor as yourself, is worth far more than all burnt offerings and sacrifices."

Jesus, seeing that he had spoken wisely, said to him, "You are not far from the kingdom of God."

THE WOMAN CAUGHT IN ADULTERY

The ancient Jewish horror of adultery is the counter-part of the ancient Jewish reverence for marriage. Most people who remember the following scene think of it in terms that would have been incomprehensible to its participants: On one side are the petty, legalistic, and bloodthirsty scholars, bent on stoning the woman for a sin that is not all that terrible, and on the other is the all-merciful Jesus. But if we are to feel the issue with the seriousness that a first-century Jew would have felt, it would be more appropriate for us to imagine the scholars bringing forward a man who had just raped and murdered a six-year-old girl. How would we react if, in this instance too, Jesus said, "Let whoever of you is sinless be the first to throw a stone at him," or, "Go now, and don't do it again"?

The next morning, as Jesus was teaching in the Temple, some scholars brought a woman who had been caught betraying her husband by having sex with another man, and they stood her in the middle. They said to him, "Rabbi, this woman was caught in adultery, in the very act of betraying her husband. Moses in the Torah commanded us to stone such women to death; what do *you* say?"

Jesus stooped down and with his finger wrote on the ground.

As they continued to question him, he stood up and said to them, "Let whoever of you is sinless be the first to throw a stone at her." Again he stooped down and wrote on the ground.

When they heard this, they went out one by one, the older ones first. Jesus was left alone, with the woman still standing there.

Jesus stood up, and said to her, "Woman, where are they? Has no one condemned you?"

She said, "No one, sir."

Jesus said, "I don't condemn you either. Go now, and never commit a crime again."

THE ARREST OF JESUS

We don't know much about Jesus' arrest and trial, or even if there *was* a trial. We do know that Pontius Pilate, the governor of Judea who sentenced Jesus to death, was a very cruel man. The Gospels try to whitewash him. According to them, he was a good man who was somehow bullied by a bloodthirsty Jewish mob into condemning Jesus to death. But the Gospels are known to have an anti-Semitic bias. Their authors were all influenced by the desire to blame the Jews for Jesus' death and to excuse the Romans. In fact, Pilate is described by Philo, a great Jewish philosopher of the time, as "naturally inflexible and stubbornly relentless, and given to acts of corruption, pillaging, outrages on the people, arrogance, repeated murders of innocent victims, and constant savagery." Pilate was finally dismissed as governor for a brutal massacre of Samaritans.

The only thing we really know about Jesus' death is that he was crucified by the Romans. The story says, "Above his head the charge against him was written: THE KING OF THE JEWS." This shows that the Romans executed him for being a rebel.

The Gospels say that the Jewish chief priests plotted to have Jesus arrested, then brought him to the Romans to be killed. (The chief priests were a small but influential Jewish aristocratic group who got their power by collaborating with the Romans.) This account may very well be true. The chief priests may have heard the rumors that this man was the Messiah, the legendary king of the Jews. Certainly they were aware that he was a dynamic teacher, who was attracting large crowds before Passover, at the most crowded and therefore most dangerous time of year. This would have been reason enough to arrest him. (Herod Antipas had arrested John the Baptist for similar reasons.) The chief priests may have thought that they should kill Jesus before he gathered more followers and proved an even more serious threat to public safety.

There is one other incident that I haven't included here. The Gospels tell a story that is traditionally called "The Cleansing of the Temple." According to it, Jesus went to the Temple, which was the center of the Jewish religion of the time, the place where animals were killed for the purpose of cleansing the people and renewing their relationship with God. (Religious beliefs can be pretty strange.) Inside the Temple grounds, Jesus supposedly overturned the tables of the money changers and the seats of the merchants who sold doves for pilgrims to sacrifice.

If this incident happened, no one knows what Jesus meant by his actions. Was it a protest? But against what? Being a good Jew, Jesus would not have seen money changing and dove selling as unacceptable actions. These were necessary services to the pilgrims who were coming, some of them from far away, to make their sacrifices. (It would have been difficult for pilgrims, rich or poor, to bring their own animals.) Was it symbolic? If so, the meaning is very obscure.

But if in fact Jesus did cause this kind of uproar in the Temple grounds, that would have been a very strong reason for the chief priests to have him arrested. They would have seen him as a serious threat to their authority and to public order, perhaps even to the Temple itself. Such violence, especially around Passover, would have seemed like the act of a dangerous or insane man. If Jesus had caused a riot, Roman troops would have been brought in (as they were on other occasions), and there could easily have been a great deal of bloodshed.

In the end, because of the Gospels' anti-Semitic bias, we can't be absolutely certain that the chief priests were involved. Most good scholars think that the general outline of the Gospel accounts are true: that Jesus was arrested and condemned by the high priest, Joseph Caiaphas, and handed over to Pilate for a final sentence. Other scholars think that the Gospels' accounts of Jesus' arrest and trial are fictions from beginning to end. The one thing we can be certain of is that the Romans were responsible for his execution.

Here is the story of the actual arrest of Jesus, taken from the Gospel accounts. Of course, if all the disciples were asleep, no one could have seen or heard Jesus praying. But the story seems true enough. Jesus must have felt that he was in great danger because he was attracting such crowds, and he may have had a premonition of his coming death.

The day before Passover and the Festival of Unleavened Bread, in the evening, he came into the city with the twelve disciples, and they ate supper. After they had sung a psalm, they went out to the Mount of Olives, across the Kidron valley, to a garden called Gethsemane.

Jesus said to his disciples, "Sit here, while I pray." Going off by himself, he bowed to the ground and prayed. He said, "Abba, all things are possible for you. Take this bitter cup from me. Nevertheless, not what I want, but what you want."

When he got up from his prayer and went to the disciples, he found them asleep. He said to them, "Why are you sleeping? Couldn't you stay awake for even one hour?" They didn't know what to answer.

Suddenly a battalion of Roman soldiers came, and some officers from the chief priests, carrying swords and clubs and lanterns and torches. They seized Jesus and bound him, and took him away.

All the disciples abandoned him, and ran away.

PETER'S DENIAL

The story of Peter's denial seems genuine in its essence, whatever the precise details may have been. In the traditional versions of the story, which originate from the Gospel of Mark, Jesus predicts Peter's denial. But all reputable scholars agree that the stories of Jesus' predictions were added later by disciples who were deeply shocked and grieved by his shameful and seemingly inexplicable death. In writing that he had actually predicted these terrible events, they probably felt that they were able in a way to control the events.

Their intention was to do honor to their beloved teacher and to portray him as he must have been (not necessarily as he was).

The soldiers took Jesus to the High Priest.

Peter followed at a distance, into the High Priest's courtyard. The slaves and attendants had made a charcoal fire, because it was a cold night; and they were standing around the fire, warming themselves. Peter stood with them and warmed himself.

One of the slave-girls came out. When she saw Peter, she looked at him closely and said, "You were there too, with that fellow from Nazareth, that Jesus." But he denied it, saying, "I don't know what you're talking about."

After a while, someone else said to Peter, "You have a Galilean accent; you must be one of them."

He said, "God curse me if I know the man!" At that moment a rooster crowed. Peter went out and burst into tears.

THE CRUCIFIXION

The Romans crucified three kinds of offenders: rebellious slaves, habitual criminals, and conspirators against Roman rule. It was a very cruel form of torture. The victim was tied or nailed to a cross. Naked, thirsty, exposed to flies and insects that bored into his wounds, unable to move, perhaps with birds of prey tearing at his eyes or nose, he was left to die in excruciating pain, sometimes after days of torment. Death came by exposure, loss of blood, and asphyxiation.

If the Gospel story is accurate, Jesus died relatively soon after he was crucified. He was one of the lucky ones.

Early the next morning, the chief priests, with the elders and scribes, bound Jesus and took him away and handed him over to Pontius Pilate, the Governor. Pilate sentenced Jesus to death. He had him whipped severely, then he handed him over to his soldiers to be crucified.

They took him out to crucify him, and seized a man named Simon of Cyrene, who was passing by on his way in from the country, and made him carry the cross.

They brought Jesus to the place called Golgotha.* Some women offered him drugged wine to ease his pain, but he wouldn't take it.

At about nine o'clock they crucified him.

Above his head the charge against him was written: THE KING OF THE JEWS. With him they crucified two Zealots, one on his right and one on his left.

At about three o'clock in the afternoon, Jesus uttered a loud cry, and died.

---

*An Aramaic word that means "the place of the skull"

THE LEGEND OF THE RESURRECTION

Sometime later, Peter had an intense feeling or vision that Jesus was alive and well, in some other form or in some other realm of existence. This encouraged the rest of the disciples greatly. Still later, stories began to circulate that Jesus had come back from the dead and had appeared to Peter or to other disciples. (The earliest Gospel, Mark, has no account of a resurrection, however. The later Gospels have different and wildly conflicting accounts.) Soon everyone among the Christians, as they now called themselves, believed that Jesus had risen from the grave, appeared to the disciples, and physically ascended into the sky.

The legend of the resurrection would have surprised Jesus. He himself never taught about a resurrection from the dead, because he wasn't afraid of death. He didn't think that death was a bad thing. He trusted God with all his heart, and he knew that whatever happened had to be good, because it happened according to the will of a supremely intelligent and loving presence. His thinking about the afterlife probably would have been as follows: "If there is an afterlife, good; if there is no afterlife, that must also be good. 'Behold, it is all very good.' If it helps you to believe one thing or the other, that is fine. But it isn't necessary to believe one thing or the other. The only important thing is to trust God and to enter the kingdom of God that is inside your own heart."

Why did Jesus die? St. Paul and other early Christians believed that he "died for our sins." This is an idea that Jesus couldn't have approved of. God, as

Jesus knew, is unconditional love. God is not some tyrant who demands the blood of an innocent victim in order to forgive people's sins. God's forgiveness is always present, whenever people are ready for it.

What would Jesus have thought about his own death? In his last hours in the garden of Gethsemane (if the story is accurate), he asked God to spare him: "Father, take this bitter cup from me. Nevertheless, not what I want, but what you want." Even with all its agony, he must have accepted his death, because he knew that it was happening according to God's will, like everything else. He knew that even when things seem unfair on the surface, there is a deeper level of reality where everything is fair. He knew that everything in the world is perfect just as it is; and that even when something seems difficult or painful, it is still very good.

AFTERWORD

The authentic Jesus, as I see him, was not a divine
being (whatever that means), born of a virgin mother,
surrounded by angels and wise men, and essentially
different from all other humans. Jesus was born in the
same way as you or I. He was probably an ordinary kid
who grew up in an ordinary small town, having his
likes and dislikes, his problems and squabbles, probably brighter than most of his playmates, possibly
kinder. Perhaps—if the townspeople thought of him
as an illegitimate child—he had a more difficult time

of it than most of us. But he weathered the difficulties, learned a trade, grew up to be a fine carpenter and a fine man. At the age of about thirty, he had an extraordinary experience of waking up to the truth. For the next year or so he went around "healing" people and teaching them, in words so alive and beautiful and compelling that they have as much power today as when they first came out of his mouth. He was a man in love with God, who gave himself completely to the acts of human kindness that proceeded from that love.

At this point you may be thinking, "Jesus' teachings sound wonderful, but what good are they? What do they mean for *me*? How can I actually live them? It's hard to really love my neighbors and impossible to love my enemies. How can I love bigots and racists, for example? How can I love people when they lie to me or betray me? Maybe *Jesus* could do that, but I can't. I can't even *like* that whiny little dork in my English class or the fat slob who lives down the street."

These are questions that people have been asking for

thousands of years. The fact is that no one, not even the greatest teacher, can show you how to love. A teacher can point you in the right direction, but that's about all. "Some say that my teaching is nonsense," Lao-tzu says in the Tao Te Ching:

> Some say that my teaching is nonsense,
> Others call it lofty but impractical.
> But to those who have looked inside themselves,
> this nonsense makes perfect sense.
> And to those who put it into practice,
> this loftiness has roots that go deep.

But *how* do you look inside yourself? One way is meditation. There are many forms of meditation: Buddhist, Hindu, Christian, nondenominational. The simplest method is to count your breaths from one to ten, then to start at one again. You may want to spend five or ten minutes meditating like this. If you like it, it will be helpful to do it every day.

Another way to look inside yourself—a way that is nondenominational and that some people find more powerful than meditation—is called The Work of Byron Katie. Instructions on how to use the four questions and turnaround are available at www.thework.com, where you can also download Byron Katie's Little Book.

Whatever method you find, when you're able to look inside yourself deeply and understand your own mind, your life will become more peaceful. And when you are feeling peaceful, it's much easier to be kind and loving. So the best way to follow Jesus' teachings is not to follow them at all but to live them. When you're able to look inside yourself deeply, you'll find that the teacher who taught Jesus will teach you. That teacher has no name. It is closer to you than breathing, nearer than your own thoughts.

NOTES

This section is addressed to parents, teachers, librarians, and young people who seek clarification on certain points in the text. For fuller clarification, you may want to read *The Gospel According to Jesus* (HarperCollins, 1991).

p. xx, *which dates from around the year 70*: The probable dates of the four Gospels are: Mark, 65–70 C.E.; Matthew, c. 80–85; Luke, c. 85–90; John, c. 100. It seems to me certain that Matthew and Luke used the text (or *a* text) of Mark's Gospel as one source of their versions. But the relationship among the three is very complex. The best introduction to the subject is E. P. Sanders and Margaret Davies, *Studying the Synoptic Gospels* (Trinity Press International, 1989).

p. xx, *except for one word,* abba: Mark has preserved two other Aramaic phrases: *"Talitha, koum"*—i.e., *"T'litha, koomi"* ("Little girl, get up," 5:41)—and *"Ephphatha"*—i.e., *"Ethpatakh"* ("Be opened," 7:34). But these may have originated in the healings and exorcisms performed by the Jewish Christians of the Jerusalem church, whereas for *abba* we have the testimony not only of Mark 14:36 ("Abba, all things are possible for you") but also of Romans 8:15 and Galatians 4:6, two of the rare instances in which Paul shows an awareness of traditions about the actual Jesus.

Some scholars think that *abba* is the familiar form, the equivalent of our *papa* or *daddy*; other scholars disagree. Our knowledge of first-century Jewish Aramaic is too limited to know which opinion is correct.

p. xxi, *"There is internal evidence"*: From a letter to John Adams, January 24, 1814.

p. xxiv, *"Among the sayings and discourses"*: From a letter to William Short, April 13, 1820.

p. 3, *people who believed some things that he himself never believed*: The essence of the Christian faith as expressed by Paul—"Christ died for our sins, was buried, and rose again on the third day" (I Corinthians 15:3–4)—would have been incomprehensible to Jesus.

p. 4, *"Wolves and lambs shall feed together"*: Isaiah 65:25.

p. 4, *referred to himself as a prophet*: Mark 6:4 (also Luke 13:33, though the authenticity of this verse is doubtful). There are also several indications that he was regarded as a prophet by people who were receptive to his teachings (Mark 6:15, 8:28, Matthew 21:11, Luke 7:16, 39).

p. 4, *he never thought of himself as the Messiah or as* the *son of God*: These two terms are ideas about Jesus that arose in the thinking of the early Church. Jesus never refers to himself that way in the Gospels of Mark, Matthew, or Luke. In the added material, however, demons, disciples, and the evangelists do designate him by these terms (Mark 1:1, 3:11, 5:7, 15:39; Matthew 4:3, 6, 8:29, 14:33, 16:16, 26:63, 27:40, 43, 54; Luke 1:32, 35, 4:3, 9, 41, 8:28, 22:70).

In the Gospel of John, on the other hand, Jesus' being "the only-begotten son of God" is a central concept from beginning to end. But John is an apologetic text, which was written to prove a theological point, and has very little to do with the actual Jesus of Nazareth. (It is also the most viciously anti-Semitic text in the New Testament.)

p. 5, *then you are a son of God*: This same sense of *son* or *child* of God, and of *begotten* as meaning "spiritually reborn," occurs in the Epistles, side by side with the later, Christological sense. We find it in the following passages:

To all who received him [the Word] and believed in his name, he gave the ability to become children of God— those who were begotten [born], not by blood, nor by the will of the flesh, nor by the will of a male, but by God (John 1:12f.).

All who are led by the spirit of God are sons of God (Romans 8:14).

In Christ Jesus I have begotten you through the Gospel (I Corinthians 4:15).

I appeal to you about my child Onesimus, whom I have begotten in prison (Philemon 1:10).

Of his own will he [God] gave birth to us by a word of truth (James 1:18, where the image is of a mother rather than a father).

Praised be the God and Father of our Lord Jesus Christ, who in his great mercy has begotten us anew into a living hope (I Peter 1:3).

See how great the love is that the Father has given us, so that we may be called children of God (I John 3:1).

We know that everyone begotten by God does not sin (I John 5:18).

And finally in Galatians 4:6, one of the most sincere and moving statements that Paul ever made:

And because [or, to show that] you are sons, God has sent forth the spirit of his son into our hearts, crying, "Abba! Father!"

p. 5, *"Blessed are the peacemakers"*: Matthew 5:9.

p. 5, *"Love your enemies"*: Matthew 5:44–45.

p. 8, *"Pray for the welfare of the empire"*: From *Pirkey Avot* (sometimes translated as *The Ethics of the Fathers*).

p. 8, *"Give to Caesar"*: Matthew 22:21.

p. 11, *Nazareth*: The Gospel of Mark provides no information about Jesus' birthplace; it just says that "Jesus came from Nazareth in Galilee." The legend that he was born in Bethlehem occurs only in the infancy legends in Matthew and Luke. Both authors thought that since Jesus was the Messiah, and since it had been prophesied that the Messiah would be born in Bethlehem (Micah 5:2), Jesus must have been born in Bethlehem. But since it was well known that Jesus came from Nazareth, they created mutually contradictory explanations. According to Matthew, Joseph and Miriam were living in Bethlehem when Jesus was conceived; after his birth, an angel in a dream warned Joseph of Herod's (unhistorical) massacre of the children, and they fled to Egypt. When they returned to Israel after Herod's death, another dream angel warned Joseph to move to Nazareth, and that explains why Jesus grew up there. But according to Luke, Joseph and Miriam were living in Nazareth. Just before Miriam was due to give birth, they had to travel to Bethlehem, Joseph's ancestral town, for the (unhistorical) census called for by the emperor Augustus, and that explains why Jesus was born there. Shortly after his circumcision, they returned to Nazareth.

p. 11, *Some scholars think that he was an illegitimate child*: See Jane Schaberg, *The Illegitimacy of Jesus* (Harper & Row, 1987).

p. 11, *trades like this were usually hereditary*: See C. H. Dodd, *The Founder of Christianity* (Collins, 1970), p. 120.

p. 14, *was baptized by him in the Jordan River*: Mark or his source, followed by Matthew and Luke, heavily mythologizes this incident: sky opening, spirit descending in the form of a dove, heavenly voice acknowledging Jesus as the divine Son.

p. 14, *All the Gospel writers were troubled by this incident*: For one thing, they were embarrassed by Jesus' subordination to John, which they explain in a variety of ways. But the issue of sin was even more embarrassing. As Mark says, "All the people were baptized by [John] in the river Jordan, confessing their sins." If Jesus was "a man without sin," as the later, and probably the early, disciples thought—or even more, if he was the preexistent Son of God—how could he have had any sins to confess, and why did he feel the need for baptism?

The evangelists dealt with the problem by immediately focusing attention on Jesus' vision (according to Mark, followed by Matthew, only Jesus could see the dove; Luke implies that everyone present could see it; according to John, it was visible only to the Baptist). The writer of the Gospel of the Nazoreans, which probably dates from the early second century, acknowledges the problem by denying the baptism:

The mother of the Lord and his brothers said to him, "John the Baptist baptizes for the forgiveness of sins; let us go and be baptized by him."

But Jesus said to them, "What sin have I committed, that I should go and be baptized by him? Unless what I just said is a sin of ignorance."

p. 25, *there are also true healers*: Western medicine, though it is right to be skeptical about traditional methods of healing, can be arrogant and dismissive of everything that the rational mind can't fit into its small categories. Nowadays, however, this mind-set is becoming a bit more open, and some of the great American schools of medicine have begun to teach Chinese and other alternative modes of healing.

Whatever the explanation of his gift, no reputable scholar doubts that Jesus was able to perform at least some of the healings attributed to him.

p. 27, *Most scholars agree*: "Few scholars think that the stories about Jesus' healings are accurate in all details, but some of the stories probably derive from reports of 'cures' that actually occurred in Jesus' presence and were understood by the patients, the observers, and Jesus himself, as miracles performed by him.

"Such cures made Jesus famous. To understand their importance, we must remember that ancient Israel had no hospitals or insane asylums. The sick and insane had to be cared for by their families, in their homes. The burden of caring for them was often severe and sometimes, especially in cases of violent insanity, more than the family could bear—the afflicted were turned out of doors and left to wander like animals. This practice continued to the present century.

"I shall never forget my first experience in the Old City of Jerusalem in 1940. The first thing I saw as I came through the

Jaffa Gate was a lunatic, a filthy creature wearing an old burlap bag with neck and armholes cut through the bottom and sides. He was having a fit. It seemed to involve a conversation with some imaginary being in the air in front of him. He was pouring out a flood of gibberish while raising his hands as if in supplication. Soon he began to make gestures, as if trying to protect himself from blows, and howled as if being beaten. Frothing at the mouth, he fell to the ground on his face, lay there moaning and writhing, vomited, and had an attack of diarrhea. Afterwards he was calmer, but lay in his puddles of filth, whimpering gently. I stood where I had stopped when I first saw him, some fifty feet away, rooted to the spot, but nobody else paid any attention. There were lots of people in the street, but those who came up to him merely skirted the mess and walked by. He was lying on the sidewalk in front of a drugstore. After a few minutes a clerk came out with a box of sawdust, poured it on the puddles, and treated the patient with a couple of kicks in the small of the back. This brought him to his senses and he got up and staggered off, still whimpering, rubbing his mouth with one hand and his back with the other. When I came to live in the Old City I found that he and half a dozen like him were familiar figures.

"Such was ancient psychotherapy. Those not willing to put their insane relatives into the street had to endure them at home. Also, since rational medicine (except for surgery) was rudimentary, lingering and debilitating diseases must have been common, and the victims of these, too, had to be cared for at home. Accordingly, many people eagerly sought cures, not only for themselves, but also for their relatives. Doctors were inefficient, rare, and expensive. When a healer appeared—a man who could perform miraculous cures, and who did so for nothing!—he was sure to be mobbed. In the crowds that swarmed around him desperate for cures, cures were sure to occur. With each cure, the reputation of his powers, the expectations and speculations of the crowd, and the legends and rumors about him would grow" (Morton Smith, *Jesus the Magician* [Harper & Row, 1968], pp. 8ff.).

p. 28, *Jesus' experience of healing may have been*: I have taken this inside view from the account of a contemporary healer. See *The Gospel According to Jesus*, Appendix 2.

p. 29, *examples of spontaneous healing*: See Caryle Hirshberg and Marc Ian Barasch, *Remarkable Recovery: What Extraordinary Healings Tell Us About Getting Well and Staying Well* (Riverhead, 1995); and Andrew Weil, M.D., *Spontaneous Healing* (Knopf, 1995).

p. 35, *people who held the law in contempt*: Literally, "tax collectors and sinners." In a present-day context, neither term has much of a sting to it: Our tax collectors are law-abiding citizens, and a "sin" can mean something as trivial as not going to church on Sunday. But in Jesus' time, the words referred to hardened criminals, whose sins would have shocked and disgusted any decent person.

"The word 'sinners' in English versions of the Bible translated the Greek word *hamartoloi*. Behind *hamartoloi* stands, almost beyond question, the Hebrew word *resha'im* (or the Aramaic equivalent). It is best translated 'the wicked,' and it refers to those who sinned wilfully and heinously and who did not repent. . . . 'Tax-collectors' were traitors. More precisely, they were quislings, collaborating with Rome. The wicked equally betrayed the God who redeemed Israel and gave them his law. There was no neat distinction between 'religious' and 'political' betrayal in first-century Judaism" (E. P. Sanders, *Jesus and Judaism* [Fortress Press, 1985], pp. 177ff.).

We might even say that Jesus' particular mission was to reform what was the first-century equivalent of the Mafia: "Those Jews who collaborated with the Roman tax-farmers by acting for them as tax-gatherers were regarded as criminals, and specifically as robbers. This was because many of the taxes were regarded as unjust . . . and the methods of tax-collecting were often cruelly oppressive. Philo describes the tortures used by tax-collectors in Egypt. . . . Since the tax-farmers had bought the tax-concession, they were allowed to exact as much as they could extort from the people. Their violence and menaces forced many citizens into outlawry, both in Palestine and Egypt" (Hyam Maccoby, *Early Rabbinic Writings* [Cambridge University Press, 1988], pp. 142f.).

p. 35, *"Why do you spend time with prostitutes and traitors?"*: Whitman, in "Song of Myself," wonderfully conveys Jesus' spirit of inclusiveness:

> This is the meal pleasantly set....this is the meat and
> drink for natural hunger,
> It is for the wicked just the same as the righteous....
> I make appointments with all,
> I will not have a single person slighted or left away,
> The keptwoman and sponger and thief are hereby
> invited....the heavy-lipped slave is invited....the
> venerealee is invited,
> There shall be no difference between them and the rest.

It is essential to understand that what is at issue here is *association* with the wicked, not *forgiveness* of the wicked. The traditional Christian view falsifies the issue, as Professor Sanders forcefully points out: "The position is basically this: *We* (the Christians, or the true Christians) believe in grace and forgiveness. Those religious qualities *characterize* Christianity, and thus could not have been present in the religion from which Christianity came. Otherwise, why the split? But the Jews, or at least their leaders, the Pharisees, did not believe in repentance and forgiveness. They not only would not extend forgiveness to their own errant sheep, they would kill anyone who proposed to do so.

"The position is so incredible that I wish it were necessary only to state it in order to demonstrate its ridiculousness. But thousands believe it, and I shall try to show what is wrong with it. Let us focus first on the *novelty* of an offer of forgiveness. The tax collectors and sinners, [the scholar Norman] Perrin assures us, 'responded in glad acceptance' to Jesus' saying that they would be forgiven. But was this news? Did they not know that if they renounced those aspects of their lives which were an affront to God's law, they would have been accepted with open arms? Is it a serious proposal that tax collectors and the wicked longed for forgiveness, but could not find it within ordinary Judaism? That they thought that only in the messianic age could they find forgiveness, and thus responded to Jesus 'in glad acceptance'? Perrin, citing only irrelevant evidence, asserts that the 'sinners' 'were widely regarded as beyond hope of penitence or forgiveness,' and thus he denies one of the things about Judaism which everyone should know: there was a universal view that forgiveness is *always* available to those who return to the way of the Lord" (*Jesus and Judaism*, p. 202).

The point of the present passage is that the scribes were shocked at Jesus' association with the wicked; being ordinary pious people, they thought that it was dangerous and futile to mix with such characters. Their attitude was exactly the same as that of Paul and the early church—for example, "Have nothing to do with any fellow-Christian who is a fornicator or a greedy man" (I Corinthians 5:11); "Do not mix with unbelievers" (II Corinthians 6:14).

The most useful commentary on this aspect of Jesus' teaching is from the twenty-seventh chapter of the Tao Te Ching:

> The Master is available to all people
> and doesn't reject anyone.
> He is ready to use all situations
> and doesn't waste anything.
> This is called embodying the light.
>
> What is a good man but a bad man's teacher?
> What is a bad man but a good man's job?
> If you don't understand this, you will get lost,
> however intelligent you are.
> It is the great secret. (Stephen Mitchell, *Tao Te Ching: A New English Version* [HarperCollins, 1988])

This is a question not of conscience but of vision. Because the Master's vision comes from beyond good and bad, he can love the essential humanity in all people, and he can see the good within the bad. He doesn't *do* anything to help others; in simply being himself, he is helping them in the best possible way.

Jesus' attitude, and Lao-tzu's, are rare. It takes great maturity to stay centered when everyone around you is lost in selfishness. It also takes great compassion. "To pull someone out of the mud," the Hasidic master Israel Baal Shem Tov said, "you must step into the mud yourself."

p. 40, *"When his family heard [about all this]"*: Mark 3:21. The Greek phrase that I have translated as "his family" means "those with him" and might also be translated "his friends" or "his relatives." But it is clear that this verse has a sequel in Mark 3:31ff. and therefore that it refers to Jesus' mother and brothers.

"they went to seize him": The Greek verb is a strong one and is used later in Mark of the troops in Gethsemane, with the meaning "to arrest."

"'He is out of his mind'": The Greek verb means "to be beside oneself," "to lose one's mind," "to be possessed."

This is one of the most hair-raising verses in the Gospels. Hidden inside it is a world of misunderstanding and disappointment. Actually, it is a miracle that the verse survived at all, to speak to us. It appears only in Mark; both Matthew and Luke apparently found it so shocking that they deleted it from their accounts. (Even in Mark, the transcribers of two of the best ancient manuscripts were so embarrassed by it that they altered it to read, "And when *the scribes and the others* [italics added] heard about him, they went to seize him, for they said, 'He is out of his mind.'")

p. 40, *the strange sounds Jesus had uttered*: According to Morton Smith, "Magicians who want to make demons obey often scream their spells, gesticulate, and match the mad in fury" (*Jesus the Magician*, p. 32).

p. 50, *righteousness*: Jesus, like other Jewish prophets, doesn't use this word in a moralistic sense. By a "righteous man" he means someone whose whole being is illuminated in God's light and who therefore naturally acts with justice and compassion.

p. 54, *Our Father in heaven*: I have used Matthew's version of the Lord's Prayer because it is such a familiar and beloved part of our Western religious tradition. Luke's version (11:2ff.), which may be more authentic, is as follows:

Father,
>   hallowed be your name.
>
> May your kingdom come.
>
> Give us each day our daily bread,
>   and forgive us our sins
>   for we ourselves forgive all those who have
>   wronged us.
>
> And do not lead us into temptation.

p. 57, *"Don't judge"*: This doesn't mean that we shouldn't see people clearly or recognize where they and we stand in the moral and spiritual realm. That kind of judgment is as necessary to compassionate action as headlights are to night driving. What Jesus means here is that we shouldn't accuse or condemn, that we should keep our hearts open to everyone. Lao-tzu explains:

> The Tao doesn't take sides;
> it gives birth to both good and evil.
> The Master doesn't take sides;
> she welcomes both saints and sinners. (*Tao Te Ching: A New English Version*, chapter 5)

The Master imitates the Tao in being available to everyone. Because she can see into the essential nature of every being, she doesn't get trapped inside her own judgments or delude herself into thinking that people *are* good or evil.

p. 58, *"What good is it for someone to say"*: This is one of two passages that I have included in Jesus' teachings that are taken from later church writings. It is from the Epistle of James, and is very much in keeping with the spirit of Jesus.

What good is it, my dear friends, for someone to say that he has faith when he doesn't act as if he loves God? Can his faith save him? If a fellow human being is naked and hungry, and you say to him, "Keep warm, eat well," and don't give him what he needs, what good is that? So faith, if it doesn't lead to action, is dead. (James 2:14ff.)

p. 61, *"Miriam's bastard"*: Literally, "the son of Mary." In English, "the son of Mary" gives no idea of the phrase's connotation in Aramaic or Hebrew. In Semitic usage, a man was normally called "[name] son of [father's name]"; if he was called "[name] son of [mother's name]," it indicated that his father was unknown and that he was illegitimate. According to a later Jewish legal principle, "A man is illegitimate when he is called by his mother's name, for a bastard has no father." "The name Yeshu ben Miriam [Jesus son of Mary] was thought to be such an unbearable insult by the early church that only Mark had the courage to retain it. All the other Evangelists omitted it" (Ethelbert Stauffer, "Jeschu ben Mirjam," in *Neotestamentica et Semitica*, ed. E. E. Ellis and M. Wilcox [Clark, 1969], pp. 119ff.).

p. 61, *"A prophet is not rejected"*: Mark 6:4. The King James Version softens the Greek by translating it "a prophet is not without honor." But the adjective means "dishonored" and derives from a verb that means "to dishonor, disgrace, shame, humiliate, treat with contempt."

This saying probably circulated independently; its form in another collection of sayings called the Oxyrhynchus Papyri is "A prophet is not accepted in his native town, nor can a doctor heal those who know him." This may be a more primitive form. On the other hand, it is unlikely that Mark added "and in his own family and in his own house"; the first of these phrases was difficult enough that Matthew omitted it.

p. 61, *"Nothing external can disturb us"*: Epictectus: *Encheiridion*, V.

p. 62, *"He lets all things come and go"*: *Tao Te Ching: A New English Version*, chapter 55.

p. 68, *"For even . . . the prophets"*: I have taken the text here from the almost entirely lost Gospel of the Nazoreans.

p. 70, *Now a priest*: The Torah says that priests and Levites—assistant priests—must not touch dead bodies. "The injured man appeared to be dead, and the priest and the Levite are represented as wishing to avoid contracting corpse impurity. . . . The priest and the Levite are not accused of lack of piety, or of self-service, but of choosing the wrong pious activity. The worship of God would go on even though one priest and one Levite were unable to share in it for a week. In this and similar circumstances the right thing to do was to care for one's brother" (E. P. Sanders and Margaret Davies, *Studying the Synoptic Gospels*, p. 182).

Samaritan: "The relations between the Jews and the mixed peoples, which had undergone considerable fluctuations, had become very much worse in the time of Jesus, after the Samaritans, between A.D. 6 and 9 at midnight, during a Passover, had defiled the Temple court by strewing dead men's bones; as a result irreconcilable hostility existed between the two parties" (Joachim Jeremias, *The Parables of Jesus*, trans. S. H. Hooke [Charles Scribner's Sons, 1955], p. 204).

p. 70, *oil and wine*: "The oil would mollify, the wine would disinfect" (ibid.).

p. 80, *"no one is perfectly good except God alone"*: Literally, "no one is good except one: God." This verse goes so much against the grain of the evangelists' desire to portray Jesus as "sinless" that it must be authentic.

By *good* Jesus means "absolutely good; perfect." This is a touchingly clear statement of how he thought of himself: as fully human and no more than human, as fully capable of making mistakes. The great English poet and painter William Blake said, "It is not because angels are holier than men or devils that makes them angels, but because they do not expect holiness from one another but from God only" ("A Vision of the Last Judgment").

In order to teach people that they all are sons of God, you have to realize that you are the son of God, but in order to teach people that they are only human, you have to realize that you are only human. What makes someone a master is not that he never makes mistakes but that when he makes a mistake, he doesn't *cling* to it.

Matthew (19:16f.) apparently found Jesus' statement so embarrassing that he changed these verses to read: "'Rabbi, what good must I do to have eternal life?' And he said to him, 'Why do you ask me about the good? There is One who is good.'" In his effort to make the verses acceptable, Matthew has turned them into nonsense, since the final sentence has no connection with the preceding one.

p. 81, *A second rich man*: This is the second passage from later church writings that I have included as an authentic teaching of Jesus. It is from the Gospel of the Nazoreans.

p. 84, *"Let the dead bury their dead"*: The most generous interpretation of this saying (we have to stretch it and disregard its harsh tone) would take it beyond the context of funerals: "Of course, your duty is to go bury your father, and you should honor him as best you can. But you shouldn't lose yourself in your grief, like those who don't know any better. Death is just a transition, as is life. Beyond life and death is true life, the only reality. That is what you should be centered in, at every moment, whether your father has just died or you have just gotten married."

p. 93, *with his finger wrote on the ground*: Scholars and theologians have debated the meaning of this action since the fourth century, and no one has come up with a convincing explanation. Perhaps Jesus was simply musing. Or perhaps the action was a vivid enactment of his feeling that all judgments are as insubstantial as words written in the dust.

This is the only Gospel scene in which Jesus is asked to act as a judge. He unequivocally refuses, thus practicing what he preached in the Sermon on the Mount.

p. 95, *Pontius Pilate*: Procurator (governor) of Judea from 26 to 36 C.E.

p. 95, *The Gospels try to whitewash him*: They all describe him as a decent fellow who believed in Jesus' innocence. Matthew's account, which is the most anti-Semitic, even adds Pilate's famous handwashing.

p. 95, *somehow bullied by a bloodthirsty Jewish mob*: "Whatever Pilate's reason for deciding to have Jesus put to death, it is not true that the Jewish crowds shouted out that Jesus should be crucified (Mark 15:12ff.) or that they took his blood upon themselves and their children (Matthew 27:25). Nor did the chief priests tell the prefect, 'We have no king but Caesar' (John 19:15). These sentences, which were later written into the account of Jesus' passion, are the products of a bitter polemic between early Christianity and Judaism and have helped to cause the horrors of two millennia of anti-Semitism" (Thomas Sheehan, *The First Coming: How the Kingdom of God Became Christianity* [Random House, 1986], p. 87).

As for the Barabbas episode, "When viewed objectively, as a reported transaction between a Roman governor, who was supported by a strong military force, and native magistrates and a native mob, the whole account is patently too preposterous and too ludicrous for belief. . . . Such an absurd presentation can be adequately explained in one way only: it resulted from Mark's concern to remove [for his Roman Christian readers] the scandal of the Roman crucifixion of

Jesus. His purpose throughout the Barabbas episode is clearly twofold: to show that Pilate recognized the innocence of Jesus; and to exonerate Pilate from responsibility for the crucifixion of Jesus by representing him as compelled by the Jewish leaders and people to order the execution. Mark appears to invoke the episode, as a kind of desperate expedient, to explain away the intractable fact of the Roman cross after he had done all he could in emphasizing the evil intent of the Jewish leaders. . . . [Matthew emphasized Jewish guilt even more and made the Jews] exclusively guilty of the awful deed. But he little knew, when he represented them as eagerly shouting: 'His blood be upon us, and on our children!,' what a terrible legacy he was thus imposing upon subsequent generations of his own people. For those fierce words came to be enshrined in the sacred scriptures of the Christian Church, where they were seen as the self-confession of the Jews to the murder of Christ. In the succeeding centuries, down to this present age, those words have inspired hatred for the Jews and justified their cruellest persecutions. (It was only during a session of the Second Vatican Council in 1965 that the Roman Catholic Church formally exonerated subsequent generations of Jews from responsibility for the murder of Christ; even then the decree met with certain opposition)" (S. G. F. Brandon, *The Trial of Jesus of Nazareth* [Stein and Day, 1968], pp. 98, 100, 115).

p. 95, *Their authors were all influenced*: "The Gospels are all influenced by the desire to incriminate the Jews and exculpate the Romans" (Sanders, *Jesus and Judaism*, p. 300).

p. 96, *Philo*: In *Legatio ad Gaium*, 301, 302.

p. 96, *The Gospels say that the Jewish chief priests*: It is possible that the priestly authorities were the motivating force behind Jesus' arrest and execution. It is also possible that the Romans arrested him as a preventive measure, without any urging from the priests. Compare the Jewish historian Josephus's account of the arrest of John the Baptist: "To some Jews the destruction of Herod's army seemed to be divine vengeance, and certainly a just vengeance, for his treatment of John, surnamed the Baptist. For Herod had put him to death, though he was a good man and had exhorted the Jews to lead righteous lives, to practice justice toward their fellows and piety toward God, and so doing to join in baptism. . . . When others too joined the crowds about him, because they were aroused to the highest degree by his sermons, Herod became alarmed. Eloquence that had so great an effect on mankind might lead to some form of sedition, for it looked as if they would be guided by John in everything that they did. Herod decided therefore that it would be much better to strike first and be rid of him before his work led to an uprising, than to wait for an upheaval, get involved in a difficult situation and see his mistake. Though John, because of Herod's suspicions, was brought in chains to Machaerus, the stronghold that I previously mentioned, and there put to death, yet the verdict of the Jews was that the destruction visited upon Herod's army was a vindication of John, since God saw fit to inflict such a blow on Herod" (Josephus, *Jewish Antiquities*, in *Works*, vol. 9, trans. Louis H. Feldman [Harvard University Press, 1965], pp. 81ff.).

If the priests were in fact responsible for Jesus' arrest, their motivation would have been more or less as the evangelists imagine it: "It was now two days before the Passover and the festival of Unleavened Bread. And the chief priests and the elders gathered in the palace of the High Priest, whose name was Caiaphas. And they said, 'What should we do? This man Jesus has performed many miracles. If we let him continue like this, everyone will follow him, and the Romans will come and take away our position and our country.' So they began to make plans to arrest Jesus secretly, for they said, 'Not during the festival, or there will be a riot among the people'" (Mark 14:1; Matthew 26:3; John 11:47f.; Mark 14:1f.).

"The story is fictitious in detail but true in essence to the situation . . . [and perfectly sums up] the problem posed for

the priests by Jesus, his followers, and their enthusiasm. . . .
The Romans, ruling central and southern Palestine at this
time, watched [the Temple] as a possible center of trouble,
and kept an eye on the rest of the country, intervening with
military force to disperse assemblies they thought dangerous. If the Temple were to become the center of a general
Jewish uprising, they might close or even destroy it. (It did
so in A.D. 66, and was destroyed in 70.)" (Smith, *Jesus the
Magician*, p. 17).

Mark (15:7), using pro-Roman language, mentions that a
"rebellion," in which a number of "rebels" had committed
"murder," had taken place just before or during Jesus' last
days in Jerusalem.

p. 100, *Suddenly a battalion of Roman soldiers came*: I have left
Judas out of this scene. There is an early tradition in which
Judas *wasn't* a traitor: Matthew 19:28 includes him on one
of the twelve thrones, judging the tribes of Israel; and in
I Corinthians 15:5, Paul says that the resurrected Jesus
"appeared to Kephas, then to the Twelve." The story of the
betrayal, which is probably later, may have been influenced
by Psalm 41:9 ("Even my friend, whom I trusted, who ate at
my table, / exults in my misfortune"), which John 13:18
quotes as a fulfilled prophecy.

"The later Christians had to explain that Jesus knew all

along, or at least in advance, that Judas would betray him (Matthew 26:25, John 6:64, 71 and frequently in John). . . . Luke and Matthew handle the embarrassment caused by Judas' defection differently, Matthew attributing foreknowledge to Jesus and restricting the number of those who saw the resurrection, Luke simply deleting the damaging part of the one saying which presupposes the continuation of the twelve around Jesus" (Sanders, *Jesus and Judaism*, p. 100).

We know very little about Judas, except that he was one of the twelve apostles and that he was called Iscariot (explanations of this name are all more or less unsatisfactory). According to John 12:1ff., after Mary, the sister of Lazarus and Martha, anoints Jesus' head at Bethany (in Mark's version of the story, the woman is nameless; in Luke's version, she is "a sinner," perhaps a prostitute), Judas protests that "the perfume could have been sold for three hundred silver coins and the money given to the poor." This is surely a legitimate concern, even a praiseworthy one. But according to John, "He said this not because he cared about the poor, but because he was a thief: he was in charge of the common purse and he used to steal what was put in it." Here the vilification of Judas has proceeded to the point where it is difficult to understand how Jesus could ever have chosen him as an apostle.

None of the evangelists provides a motivation for Judas'

treachery that is even remotely believable. Mark has him betray Jesus spontaneously and for no reason; according to Matthew, greed is the motivation, and Judas goes to the priests to trade information for money; according to Luke, he goes because Satan has entered into him. In John's Gospel too, Satan enters into Judas, but with the complicity of Jesus himself, and only after Jesus gives Judas a piece of dipped bread at the Last Supper (13:27).

p. 103, *a very cruel form of torture*: Cicero called it "that most cruel and disgusting penalty," and Josephus, "the most wretched of deaths."

p. 104, *uttered a loud cry*: According to Mark, followed by Matthew, Jesus' last words were a quotation from Psalm 22 ("My God, my God, why have you forsaken me?"); according to Luke, a quotation from Psalm 30 ("Father, into your hands I commend my spirit"). But since the disciples had scattered, it is unlikely that any of them witnessed the crucifixion. Even if they did, they would have been allowed to watch it only from a considerable distance, as Mark says of Mary Magdalene and certain other women (15:40), and they would not have been able to distinguish Jesus' words.

"Many scholars think that, like the other borrowings from Psalm 22, these words too were borrowed from the same source, not by Jesus, but by the Evangelist, or by tradition. Jesus died with a 'loud cry.' What did he say? What had he said? Pious fantasy soon found answers; hence what we now read in Mark and Luke. Jesus was the Messianic hero predicted and represented in the Psalm. Therefore, he is made to quote its opening words, not because those who put the words in his mouth thought that he was, or believed he was, forsaken of God, but because they are the opening words of the Psalm" (C. G. Montefiore, *The Synoptic Gospels* [Macmillan, 1927], vol. 1, p. 383).

p. 104, *and died*: The evangelists add an account of the burial: "And late in the afternoon, since it was Friday and the Sabbath was approaching, Joseph of Arimathea, a respected member of the Sanhedrin, who was himself looking for the kingdom of God, took courage and went to Pilate and asked him for the body of Jesus. And Pilate ordered that it be given to him. And Joseph bought a linen cloth, and took the body down, and wrapped it in the cloth. And he laid it in a tomb that had been cut in the rock. And he rolled a large stone against the door of the tomb, and departed" (Mark 15:41, Luke 23:54; Matthew 27:58; Mark 15:46; Matthew 27:60). These verses may be historical, or they may be apologetic, to prepare for the myth of the empty tomb. Some scholars think it probable that Jesus' body was taken down from the cross by the soldiers and thrown into a mass grave.

p. 105, *Peter had an intense feeling or vision*: By far the most insightful study of the "Easter experience" is Thomas Sheehan's above-mentioned book, *The First Coming*.

Briefly, what must have happened was this: Sometime after the crucifixion Peter had an experience in which he became convinced that Jesus was somehow still alive, that he had been "raised" by God. Or perhaps the experience was Mary Magdalene's, and she told it to Peter and the other apostles. It may have been a sudden realization that was later expressed in mythological terms as a physical resurrection and ascension into the sky. Or it may have been some kind of psychological phenomenon, like the many documented apparitions of what we call ghosts. Whatever it was, it lifted the apostles from the depths of their grief and from some of their guilt at having abandoned Jesus after his arrest and changed them into men and women of great courage and faith.

This transformation of the apostles is one of the cornerstones of Christian apologetics, and it is, to be sure, impressive and deeply moving. But we need to be aware of the *quality* of the transformation. It was what I would call a religious rather than a spiritual experience. That is, although it took the apostles from doubt and despair to faith, it didn't take them into the kingdom of God. "Every disciple who is fully taught will be like his teacher" (Luke 6:40). But they were nowhere near being fully taught. They only believed in, they hadn't experienced, God, and they still didn't understand Jesus' teaching. They thought that the kingdom of God was an external event and that it was still to come: soon, very soon, but in the future. At first they believed that it would certainly come within their own lifetimes (Mark 9:1, I Thessalonians 4:15ff.). As their hope was gradually disappointed, they came to believe that the kingdom would only come after death, that, as Paul said, "Flesh and blood can't inherit the kingdom of God" (I Corinthians 15:50)—i.e., you can't enter the kingdom of God while you are alive.

The gospel they preached was not the good news that Jesus had proclaimed. Instead of teaching God's presence, they preached "that Christ died for our sins, in accordance with the Scriptures; and that he was buried; and that he was raised on the third day, in accordance with the Scriptures; and that he appeared to Peter, and then to the Twelve" (I Corinthians 15:3ff.), and that he would soon return to judge the living and the dead. Instead of God's absolute love and forgiveness, they preached a god who condemned most of humankind to eternal damnation and would save only those who believed that Jesus was the Son of God.

p. 105, *The earliest Gospel, Mark, has no account of a resurrection*: Mark 16:9–20 is a later addition, which doesn't appear in the earliest and best manuscripts.

p. 111, *"Some say that my teaching is nonsense"*: *Tao Te Ching: A New English Version*, chapter 67.